"This book is like taking a cool shower after spending the day in a humid, sticky heat wave. The success culture that prizes investments more than integrity and goods more than God beats down on us like a hot sun. It can easily wear us down and seduce us to see the mirage of earthly success as true rest and joy.

"Charles and Janet Morris, modern-day Augustines, invite us to assess whether we will be citizens of the City of God or the City of Man. Their refreshing and compelling portrayal of true success will cleanse us of the foolishness of following false idols of success and provide us with the invigorating hope that our lives can achieve abundance in this life and the one to come far beyond our wildest imagination. This is a must-read for all who feel the pull of the City of Man and long to know the fresh, freeing breeze of the City of God."

Dan B. Allender, Ph.D.
Author
Mars Hill Graduate School

"Here is a breath of fresh air! With one foot in the world of the *New York Times* and the other in the text of Scripture, the Morrises, writing with refreshing candor, provide us with a clear understanding of what it means to live differently in the world. I have read this book to great personal challenge and profit."

Alistair Begg
Pastor, Parkside Church
Radio Speaker, "Truth for Life"

"Sometimes the voices of the world play with our minds. We start by knowing truth . . . but there is this incremental movement in the direction of the lies, the sham, and the pretense. It's easy to sell out. *Jesus in the Midst of Success* is an attack of sanity in an insane world. This book will remind you about who you are and Whose you are. In a refreshing and winsome way, Charles and

Janet Morris call us to remember the truth in a world of lies. You're going to love this book."

Steve Brown
Bible Teacher, "Key Life" Radio Program
Professor, Reformed Theological Seminary

"Watch out, the spiritual surgery required from *Jesus in the Midst of Success* will be both painful and liberating. The life-changing take-away value will be the ability to embrace the power of the Spirit in the marketplace of ideas and accomplishments."

Jon M. Campbell
President, Ambassador Advertising Agency

"Weaving together illustrative stories and godly wisdom, this book entertains even as it convicts."

Dr. Michael S. Horton
Author and Christian Apologist

"Charles and Janet Morris write out of an understanding that the gospel is not just the way we enter the kingdom of God. It's the center to which we must orient all our relationships and activities if we are not to fall back into a performance- or success-oriented life. *Jesus in the Midst of Success* is a challenge to our culture's equation of success with God's favor."

Dr. Tim Keller, Senior Pastor
Redeemer Presbyterian Church, New York City

"Success comes in many forms: power, wealth, notoriety. The lure is seductive; pursuing it consumes our energy. *Jesus in the Midst of Success* redirects our thoughts toward Jesus himself, in whom we find true success both in this life and beyond. I strongly recommend that you read this compelling book."

Tremper Longman III, Ph.D.
Professor, Westmont College
Author of Reading the Bible with Heart and Mind

"In these pages you'll read the fascinating stories of people captured by the one who is meek and lowly in heart. Behind the scenes you'll also meet my warm, wise friends, Charles and Janet Morris. And, most of all, you'll see Jesus! He's what it's all about."

Dr. Ray Ortlund
Author
President, Renewal Ministries

"If the church today is starving, it needs to eat this book. Many of us know the Scriptures and have good intentions, yet languish in the area of application. This book combines fascinating illustrations with winsome yet provocative guidance. A much needed plea for authenticity, *Jesus in the Midst of Success* teaches us that brokenness and weakness are to be embraced as prerequisites for true discipleship. We can build something with the "arm of flesh," but it isn't the City of God. Since we can't con the Almighty, it is best to simply follow the cross and the Christ—all the way home."

Richard A. Swenson, M.D.,
Author, Margin *and* The Overload Syndrome

JESUS

IN THE

MIDST

OF

SUCCESS

JESUS
— IN THE —
MIDST
— OF —
SUCCESS

Standing Faithful
in Seasons of Abundance

CHARLES W. MORRIS & JANET E. MORRIS

BROADMAN
& HOLMAN
PUBLISHERS

Nashville, Tennessee

© 2000 by Charles and Janet Morris
All rights reserved
Printed in the United States of America

0-8054-1978-0

Published by Broadman & Holman Publishers,
Nashville, Tennessee

Dewey Decimal Classification: 248.4
Library of Congress Card Catalog Number: 00-029271

Unless noted otherwise, Scripture quotations are from the Holy
Bible, New International Version, © 1973, 1978, 1984 by
International Bible Society. Verses marked NASB are from the New
American Standard Bible, © the Lockman Foundation, 1960, 1962,
1963, 1968, 1971, 1972, 1973, 1975, 1977, used by permission;
and TLB, The Living Bible, © Tyndale House Publishers, Wheaton,
Ill., 1971, used by permission.

Library of Congress Cataloging-in-Publication Data
Morris, Charles W., 1952–
    Jesus in the midst of success : standing faithful in seasons
of abundance / Charles W. Morris, Janet E. Morris.
        p. cm.
    ISBN 0-8054-1978-0
    1. Businesspeople—Religious life. 2. Success—Religious
aspects—Christianity. I. Morris, Janet E., 1950– II. Title.

BV4596.B8 M67   2000
248.4—dc21

                                  00-029271
2 3 4 5 04 03 02 01 00

To Jim Boice and Jack Miller,
dear teachers and friends.

Contents

Foreword xiii

Preface xvii

1. Going for the Glory 1
2. Getting Leveled 17
3. Learning to See 29
4. Leaning Hard 45
5. Being Righteous 63
6. Going Under 81
7. Living Deliberately 99
8. Weighing Truth 117
9. Taking Action 133
10. Crying "Father" 153
11. Getting Carried Away 173

Notes 193

Foreword

Let me begin by saying two things about Charles Morris, my good friend and former coworker with the Alliance of Confessing Evangelicals.

First, I have never met anyone, either in my church work or my extensive travels, who is as genuinely interested in other people as Charles is. Charles has worked with me as the announcer on the Bible Study Hour and as the host of various seminars the Alliance has offered across the United States. I have always been amazed at the number of people he knows and the detailed information about them and their families that he displays so artlessly. He remembers the names of their husbands and wives and children, how old the children are, where they go to school, and what problems they may have been having. He remembers the challenges the people face at work, and he calls them on a regular basis to find out how they are doing and to pray for them.

Charles reminds me of the apostle Paul who wrote to the church at Rome, a place he had never been, and who sent greetings to scores of people he had met and gotten to know in his missionary travels and who had since moved to the capital.

Second, I do not know of anyone who is as genuinely uninterested in success, as the world defines success, as Charles is. Charles has enormous ability as a Christian teacher, writer, and speaker, which will become increasingly evident in his new responsibilities with Haven Ministries. But he never seems to be putting himself forward or seeking for human applause or acclaim. I am sure that is because he is thinking instead about the people he is with and for whom he cares.

All of this has equipped him to write this book. It is about success as the world defines it and pursues it, often to the exclusion of all else, and as Christians have pursued it in obedience to Jesus Christ. The book is filled with much Bible knowledge and spiritual wisdom. But the personal stories of the people Charles has known are what make it so valuable and such delightful reading.

They are an amazing collection, from leaders like C. Everett Koop, the former surgeon general of the United States who is known by millions of people all over the world, to people like Gary Grauberger, a brilliant gold prospector who lives in Lake Tahoe, Nevada, but who is probably known only to a few. Charles writes about Robert G. LeTourneau, founder of the LeTourneau earthmoving equipment company; Bill McGreevy, former manager of a high-pressure gas pipeline in the Midwest who is now the chief executive officer of the Alliance of Confessing Evangelicals; Doug Cobb, the founder, former owner, and editor of *The Cobb Report;* John Weiser, who handles investment capital for the Bass Brothers in Fort Worth, Texas; Charlie Peacock, a writer and performer of Christian music; Truett Cathy, the founder of Chick-fil-A; pastors like D. Martyn Lloyd-Jones, Chuck DeBardeleben, Jim Cymbala, and Joseph Wheat; and other people, like Cecilia Chacon, Jeff Comment, John D. Beckett, Howard Butt, and Joni Eareckson Tada.

I have been privileged to know many of these people, in many cases because Charles has introduced me to them, and I can vouch for the stories and testimonies that are recorded here. These are people who have grappled with the world's definition of success but have learned to reject it, live for Jesus Christ, and seek the kind of success he requires. They have been blessed because of it.

The other author of this book is Janet, Charles's wife. I do not know Janet as well as I do Charles because I have traveled with Charles for quite a few years while Janet has usually remained at home to care for their home and children. However, I have been to their home and have been graciously received and entertained by Janet Morris. I can say this: Janet is the steady foundation that has enabled Charles to travel as extensively as he has. She has been his anchor. More than that, she is an excellent writer and an extremely hard worker. I suspect that she has had more to do with the actual writing of this valuable and provocative book than Charles.

So I commend it to you, the reader. In the fast-paced, commercially driven culture in which we live, almost everybody wants to be successful. And they should! The problem is that we often measure success by the wrong standards and, therefore, soon discover that the success we achieve is unsatisfying and sometimes even harmful both to ourselves and others. The answer to our success-driven illusions is to discover how God measures success and to try to please him.

I have been encouraged and blessed by *Jesus in the Midst of Success,* and I am sure you will be too.

James Montgomery Boice

Preface

Brian Esterly—former Gulf War marine, Wharton MBA, and now Anderson consultant—marched with competent single-mindedness toward his goal: success in the world of business. But along the way, he became a Christian. On the Sunday morning when he was formally received into the church, his pastor read this Scripture: "The world and its desires pass away, but the man who does the will of God lives forever" (1 John 2:17).

Brian was a student at the Wharton School at the time. "The world and its desires was what Wharton was all about," he says. "It's a two-year focused job search and the stated goal is to make money." Brian found himself between two colliding worlds, and he felt the tension intensely.

Brian's not alone. As Christian philosopher Jacques Ellul puts it, "the Christian belongs to two cities . . . living in this world, he belongs to another . . . the two cities to which he belongs can never coincide, and the Christian must not abandon either the one or the other . . . . Thus he is obliged to accept the tension."

We all feel that tension. And as Ellul correctly points out: only in the life of the layperson—the person in the midst of the world—will we begin to see how to live out the tension. This book is an attempt to find some honest answers to the problem we all face—the problem of living in colliding worlds. It's full of stories of real people whose lives show the glory of the City of God breaking through in the midst of the City of Man. We thank them for their transparent testimonies.

Chapter 1
Going for the Glory

*[Jesus] noticed how the guests picked the
places of honor at the table.*
LUKE 14:7

Success. It's that thing we want.

It's not just money. It's the independence of needing no one.
It's the pleasure of good things. It's the power to avoid suffering.
It's the elevation above the struggle. It's the valet opening our door.
It's the good things people say about us. It's being vindicated.

Success is an integral, taken-for-granted part of our world. A
copy of *Hustler* may be hidden in the brown paper bag, but no one
is embarrassed to buy *Success* magazine. Success comes under various guises—significance, having an impact, the good life, personal goals, having a dream, self-actualization—but everyone
wants it. Regardless of what it's called or how it's measured, success seems to determine worth and drive life.

Jeff Comment wanted it. A commanding presence, Comment
had always been a hard-driving, hard-working individual with a
unique aura that set him apart as a leader. He seemed born to be
a CEO, and in 1977 his lifelong dream was achieved when he was

named president of the Wannamaker department store chain based in Philadelphia.

"Do you remember your big promotion? The job you worked for and dreamed for all those years? The day the boss walked in and said, 'You got it!' That dream came true for me when I became president of John Wannamaker's. I had moved from Florida to Pennsylvania with one goal in mind: to be president of that company. Now I had made it. I was excited! It felt good to be president."[1]

Even before he was given the reins of the company, Comment decided he would quickly make his mark as president. "I needed to show my boss I was special and that his decision to put me in charge was a good one." So Jeff began to look for trouble spots where he could prove that he was a problem solver who takes challenges head on. He knew his credibility with his board and the Wannamaker family depended on a quick increase in profits. It didn't take long for Jeff to find a trouble spot where he could make his mark. The furniture department was not as profitable as it should have been because of poor productivity and substandard customer service. The problem, according to Comment's evaluation, was the delivery drivers who didn't seem to be making the customers a top priority. He made his first major presidential decision and canceled the contract with a trucking firm that used Teamster drivers, hiring nonunion truckers instead.

What happened next took him by surprise. "Here I was, the brash, take-charge president, making what I thought was a sound business decision that made good business sense. I never dreamed that what was about to happen would merit a chapter in the company's history. I was going to leave a mark on John Wannamaker's, all right."

Comment hadn't considered the ramifications of firing the Teamsters. He was new to Philadelphia—where the Teamsters reign, and where the Teamster leaders make their dissatisfaction over their employees being without jobs strongly felt.

The strike began, and Comment's presidential office became a war zone. "People looked to me for answers, but to be honest I didn't have a clue as to where to turn. I was crushed, humiliated, and felt totally foolish.

"The parent company was starting to question my judgment. The poor press we received didn't help. I was asked more than once why I didn't do my homework and why I hadn't anticipated this kind of problem."

In the end, after a ninety-day strike, serious property damage, several people physically injured on both sides, and a $2-million loss, a labor arbitrator brought the two parties together and nego-tiated a compromise agreement. The Teamsters were back on the trucks, but with a new third-party trucking company and a com-mitment to customer service.

Jeff was left with an identity crisis. His concept of himself had been severely shaken. He was the one who could take charge and make things happen—the one who just needed a chance to prove himself.

He ran Wannamakers for another nine years and eventually went on to become the chairman and CEO of Helzberg Diamonds—a Warren Buffet-owned Berkshire Hathaway company and the second largest jewelry chain in the U.S. But along the way, his unexamined desire for success underwent some serious revi-sion. The rest of his story will be told, but we need to stop right here and ask a fundamental question: From where does this driv-ing, taken-for-granted desire for success come?

THE GENESIS OF SUCCESS

If we go back, way back, to the very beginning, we can find the answer to that question. Open the pages of Genesis and you read of two brothers who bring an offering to the Creator. One brother brings a firstborn lamb from his flock and sacrifices it upon an altar. The other brother brings some of the crop he has just harvested. God is pleased with the lamb Abel brings, but Cain's offering is rejected. Cain takes it as a personal put-down. Even though God reasons with him that he will be accepted if he brings a right offering, Cain isn't having it. He is furious, and his wounded, burning jealousy erupts into murder.

Although we might expect God to kill Cain on the spot for killing Abel, he doesn't. He sends him away. And the record has it that Cain "went out from the LORD's presence. . . . Cain was then building a city, and he named it after his son" (Gen. 4:16–17). In response to the humiliation of being rejected by God, Cain "seeks an occasion to be prominent," as Martin Luther puts it.[2]

Hating to be put down. Scrambling to be on top. It's all there in Cain's story. While sin was first born in his parents, Cain takes it and gives it its corporate expression. Cain's drive to exalt himself and recover from his humiliation is the same fuel that drives our desire for success. We just naturally go for it.

The concept of worldliness has taken a lot of shapes in the Christian culture. We've thought of it as being synonymous with the entertainment industry or marketing or materialism. But these are just specific expressions of worldliness. The essence is the drive to be above it all—what the New Testament calls "boasting." In Galatians 6:13–14, Paul equates worldliness with boasting, and John describes worldliness as "the cravings of sinful man, the lust of his eyes and the boasting of what he has and does" (1 John 2:16). The world is not so much a place as it is a dynamic built on our impulse to indulge and exalt ourselves. In the Bible, "the world" often goes by the name of "Babylon," the city that gives herself "glory and luxury" and boasts, "I sit as queen" (Rev. 18:7).

LIVING IN TWO CITIES

The "city" theme runs through the Bible from beginning to end. Fifteen centuries ago, Augustine explained all of human history in the context of two cities that he said have existed from the genesis of man and are diametrically opposed to one another: the City of Man (Babylon or "the world") and the City of God.

"The [City of Man], in a phrase, glories in itself," Augustine explains, "the [City of God] in the Lord." That is the fundamental difference between the two cities. "The one seeks glory from men; but the greatest glory of the other is God. . . . The one lifts up its head in its own glory; the other says to its God, 'Thou art my glory, and the lifter up of mine head.'"[3]

The promise of the City of God first occurs in Genesis and continues to the closing pages of the Bible. According to Hebrews, Abel and all the generations up to the present have looked for a heavenly city whose architect and builder is God. The final two chapters of Revelation contain a description of that city as it will be when it comes into the fullness of reality. As Augustine said, "Its glory is God." The essential thing about the City of God is that God is in her midst and that he is her boast—her glory.

Jeff Comment is a citizen of the City of God, but like the rest of us, he is still *in* the City of Man. As followers of Christ, we know we are called to be *in* the world and yet not to be *of* it, but we really don't know what that means. Our consciences cringe from the compromises and rationalizations we make, but the pressures are great. We feel the constant anxiety of trying to serve two masters and still remain faithful to a single love. We live simultaneously in two diametrically opposed worlds, and we face a daily question: How can we deal with the realities of the City of Man while remaining loyal to the City of God, which is our eternal home?

That's what this book is about. Like so many things, the key is understanding. We need—first of all—to understand how the City of Man operates. We need to see the real agenda driving the world so we can operate according to another agenda. We need to get a clear picture of the glory the City of Man has been seeking since Cain went off to build his city so that we can turn and seek another glory—the glory of the City of God.

HOW THE CITY OF MAN WORKS

The bottom-line preoccupation of the City of Man is the question, Who's on top?

Glory is just another word for the thing that lifts us up or exalts us, and *shame* is just another word for being put down or abased. We hate someone to "look down" on us. We say that someone in authority is "over" us and we speak of "top/down" organizational charts. We don't want to be "put down." We talk about people who have "reached the top." And in the old sitcom song, the family exults in "movin' on up."

Our terminology reflects our intuitive understanding of the City of Man's hierarchy. The teacher is above the student. The famous are above the obscure. The judge is above the defendant. The victor is above the defeated. The young and healthy are above the old and sick. And, of course, the rich are above the poor. We instinctively strive for the top—for success. In like manner we shun the bottom—the place of the failure, of the loser. A number of other things characterize the way things work in the City of Man.

MAKING COMPARISONS

It's not just a matter of being "up," but of being "above" some-one else. Conversely, it's not so much being "down," as being "below" someone else. You drive out of the parking lot of the Toyota dealer in your new Camry, smelling the new car smell and feeling good. At the first red light an old Chevy Nova with its lus-ter of newness long gone pulls up beside you. Your Camry pulsates with glory. Then you look to the right. A sleek black Mercedes purrs in quiet superiority, its dark tinted windows enclosing the inhabitants of an exclusive world. You console yourself with thoughts of getting thirty miles to the gallon. Getting glory in the City of Man is inherently competitive.

BEING SEEN

Glory has to be seen. It's measured by the opinion of others. The City of Man is constantly in the business of conferring its judgment about who gets glory and who doesn't. The high school reunion is a microcosm of this dynamic. Back at commencement, glory has been mainly a matter of potential. Now years later, you see who has realized that potential. You exult over the prom queen who has gained fifty pounds. But woe to you if *you* were the prom queen—your fifty pounds will feel like a hundred when you fall under the scrutiny of your former classmates.

FEELING SHAME

Shame comes when we are exposed to the eyes of judgment and are found to be lacking. If nobody sees us, there is no sense of shame. When we come under scrutiny, however, we become aware of ourselves. Of course, we all know our audience includes people who see us in the arena of our imagination. Our impulse is to cover up.

We may be blissfully unaware that our socks don't match—until we cross our legs at the power lunch and realize one sock is blue and one is black. How do we react? We probably quickly put our feet down on the floor and keep them there. On the other hand, we may choose to point out the mismatch to everyone and share in the laughter rather than risk becoming the object of it.

We feel shame in the City of Man when we are seen to lack the things that humankind considers glorious. Even the prisoner of war, who has no moral reason to feel shame, cringes when his rescuers shine the flashlight into his cell and find him dirty, weak, and vermin-ridden.

The most burning shame of all comes from being treated as nonexistent—being looked through as though we're not even there. The awkward adolescent who enters the party uncertain of his acceptance and thinks for a moment he's being welcomed—only to realize that the exuberant greeting is for the person coming in behind him—feels intense shame. Being hated is better than being ignored.

DECIDING WHO COUNTS

As professor David Wells says, "Every society has its way of assessing who is important and who is not, who has value and who does not."[4] The dynamic of assigning glory is the same, but the things that constitute glory vary. In the apostle Paul's time, people were to some extent born into their station. Therefore Paul could boast of his city, Tarsus, which in the world's eyes had a significance that was bestowed on its citizens. Israel's boast was the Law, and the group that had the most to boast about in that regard were the Pharisees. Paul was a Pharisee of the Pharisees. Even by the judgment of the group judged most righteous, he was considered faultless. Paul had no small amount of glory in the City of Man.

Every subculture defines glory by its own unique criteria. Academia values success in that arena, especially if a work has been published or recognized. The Philadelphia Blue Book still bestows regard only on certain families. On the other hand, in the blue-collar Italian neighborhood of South Philly, snobby self-importance is a joke. In fact, laughing at someone is a universal mechanism for putting them down. In the Victorian age "respectability" was valuable currency, but in our day it doesn't count for very much.

Championship wrestling, Wall Street, hip-hop, your own block—every arena has a unique measurement of status. The greater the status of that subarena in the assessment of the larger culture, the greater the glory it brings to its members. We pull for a team in football; if they win the national championship, we bask in the glory. Our church is growing and we have a great preacher; we're elevated by being a part of this success. In Genesis 11 we see that the impulse to get together and build something for the glory of man is a strong motivator. In Babel, the people said to each other, "Come, let us build ourselves a city, with a tower that reaches to the heavens, so that we may make a name for ourselves" (Gen. 11:4).

INVENTING OURSELVES

Nowadays, status is more fluid than it was in the past, and it is ostensibly available to all in the modern world. That means we bear the burden of having to invent ourselves. Nothing is a given. What's more, the arena has enlarged to include the entire world, and the rules are constantly shifting. We never really know where we stand.

Paradoxically, this also enables us to find ways of elevating ourselves, at least in our own eyes. One woman may boast to her friend that she has never made a cake from a mix. Her friend listens with mild amusement as she thinks how mundane it is to be preoccupied with the kitchen.

We often seek out people who have enough savvy to recognize our brand of glory. Maybe only collectors of Beatles memorabilia will realize the importance of the George Harrison doll one owns. If you use a Montblanc pen, you can only gain status from it in the society of people who know how expensive Montblanc pens are. In the society of simple lifestylers, your Montblanc may actually become a detriment to your status.

GETTING ON THE INSIDE

Glory in the City of Man gets much of its shine from its exclusivity. Any token of privilege bestows glory. The ability to enjoy leisure and luxury elevates us. Advertisers display their products in the world of the elite. The glory that comes from being a member of the privileged few is an integral part of the dynamics of the City of Man. Knowing a famous man is good, but being a part of his intimate circle of friends is even better.

C. S. Lewis says there is a secret "hierarchy" that operates in any society, and within each hierarchy there is an inner circle. "You discover gradually, in almost indefinable ways, that it exists and that you are outside it; and then later, perhaps, that you are inside it."[5]

"Exclusion is no accident," Lewis says. "It is its essence."[6]

KICKING AGAINST THE MASTERS

Submission to authority is felt as humiliation in the City of Man. While pleasing the authorities can be the most direct route to gaining a higher place, rebellion is often a shortcut—especially for the young, who tend to feel their powerlessness intensely. Defiant anger, youthful disdain, and glorification of the repugnant (check out generation-X music for examples) are all manifestations of the glory of rebellion in the pursuit of autonomy.

BEING THE TOP OF THE TOP

Being above it all is the best place to be according to the City of Man—beyond striving, not answering to anyone, disdaining the opinions of others. Humanistic psychologist Abraham Maslow said that "striving upward" is a "widespread and perhaps universal tendency."[7] He used a hierarchy—or ladder—of needs as a model to understand human behavior. As each need on the hierarchy is satisfied (starting with the need for food and shelter), people begin to strive for the next highest need.

The top of the hierarchy—the thing everyone ultimately strives for—is something Maslow called "self-actualization." A study group of people he identified as having reached this pinnacle exhibited a "beyond judgment" self-concept. They had a relative lack of guilt, shame, or anxiety. Their ethics were "autonomous and individual."[8] They had a quality of detachment and were "ruled by the laws of their own character."[9] According to Maslow, they were "strong enough to be independent of the good opinion of other people, or even of their affection." Their seeming indifference to "the honor, the status, the rewards, the popularity, the prestige and the love" that the rest of humanity strives after came from having received such an abundance of it all their lives.[10]

Maslow was an acute observer of the dynamics of the City of Man, but his conclusions were flawed. As a humanist, he considered man to be the measure of all things. Therefore, what man seeks to be, man has a legitimate right to be. Since the "end" to which each human strives is to be autonomous—a law unto himself, answering to no one but himself—then, according to Maslow, this end must be good.

MAKING MONEY

Money is the only truly credible and universal medium of glory in the City of Man—money and the things it can purchase. The universal striving for glory takes place especially in the market-place—the heart of the City of Man—where money can be acquired and the symbols of status can be purchased. Poverty, conversely, is the universal shame—unless it's freely chosen for altruistic reasons; then it takes on the gild of self-sacrifice.

THE TROUBLE WITH MAN'S GLORY

The trouble—to put it mildly—is that God doesn't like the way the City of Man works.

When we read 1 Corinthians, we realize that Paul is writing to a church still operating, to a large extent, according to the dynamics of the City of Man. The Corinthian church had developed divisions around certain heroes. One group was claiming Peter, another Apollos, and another Paul. They were sort of basking in the glory of their group's hero and quarreling about which hero was better. Paul reproved them for giving men glory, and he asked them, "Are you not worldly? Are you not acting like mere men?" (1 Cor. 3:3)

"God chose the weak things of the world to shame the strong. He chose the lowly things of this world and the despised things—and the things that are not—to nullify the things that are, so that no one may boast before him" (1 Cor. 1:27–29), Paul says to make his point.

God has purposely reversed the hierarchy of glory that operates in the world. He has chosen to nullify it. When we *nullify* something, we cancel it. We make it *null,* which means "without value, insignificant, amounting to nothing." God has taken it upon himself to nullify the whole system of glory and shame that determines who has substance and value in the City of Man. He's doing this in several ways:

He's declaring his opinion of it. In his Word he says it over and over again. Open the Bible at random, close your eyes, point to practically any verse, and you'll get the drift. God considers all the glory of the City of Man, everything it values—all its gold, its greatest heroes, its self-importance, and its preoccupations—to be as significant as a mote. A mote is a speck of dust.

In Hebrew the word for *glory* is *kabod,* which means "weight." The things that have glory are "heavy" (as hippies used to say). But according to God, the thing we call success—the thing that gives us gravity in the City of Man—has no weight at all. In fact, God seems to find it amusingly absurd. God is the only one with glory. He has all the weight.

He's disallowing it in the City of God. In the City of Man, doors open for the successful. But entering the City of God is a different story. Our assets in the City of Man become liabilities when we seek to enter the City of God. We have to leave them at the door. If we look at ourselves through God's eyes, we will see that what we thought was wisdom is really foolishness, what we thought was important is insignificant, what we thought was wealth is valueless currency. In God's eyes we are "wretched, pitiful, poor, blind and naked" (Rev. 3:17).

He has invalidated its judgments. John starts his Gospel by saying that the "Word" (God's Son, v. 1) came "to that which was his own" and that the world "did not receive him" (v. 11). But as you keep reading, it gets worse. The system checks him out and judges him worthy—not of glory, but of the lowest place in the City of Man. In the pomp and power of the Roman Empire, the ultimate degradation was to be stripped and nailed like a carcass onto two pieces of wood. The City of Man heaped on the Son of God its most extreme scorn and, in doing so, proved that its judgments are 180 degrees off.

He's set a day when he will destroy it. On the Day of the Lord the dynamics of the City of God will prevail as the true reality, and God will stamp "canceled" on the City of Man. "The arrogance of man will be brought low / and the pride of men humbled; / the LORD alone will be exalted in that day" (Isa. 2:17).

The City of Man is in competition with the City of God. It is attempting to imitate God's wisdom and strength and honor and glory while it ignores God and goes about its business as if God does not exist. This challenge will not go unmet. According to the Bible, the City of Man is a sitting duck. In Revelation 18:7, the voice from heaven pronounces judgment on the City of Man: "Give her as much torture and grief as the glory and luxury she gave herself."

THE GLORY OF THE CITY OF GOD

Does this sound depressing? Actually it might because there is something missing, something very important. Augustine said that the glory of the City of God is God. This doesn't only mean that God gets all the glory. It also means that God *is* the glory of his people.

The City of Man's "craving for undue exultation" happens— according to Augustine—"when the soul abandons Him to whom it ought to cleave as its end, and becomes a kind of end in itself. . . . It becomes its own satisfaction."[11] As citizens of the City of God, God is our glory, not ourselves. He lifts us up by giving us himself. He is ours and we are his. His love is our value, our status, our identity, our satisfaction, our glory.

When we "weigh" the glory we have as members of the City of God, it gives us an accurate assessment of the glory and the shame we experience in the City of Man. Paul lists his City-of-Man assets in Philippians 3:5–6, and they are weighty. Before his conversion they constituted his identity and, like Jeff Comment's success, defined his significance. But Paul says that these things that were to his profit, he now considers "a loss" compared to the "surpassing greatness" of knowing Christ Jesus his Lord. He says something very similar about his humiliations in 2 Corinthians 4:17 and Romans 8:18. Paul went from being honored in the world to being treated like scum. He didn't even get much respect in the church for his apostleship. But Paul dismissed these things as "light" because they were far outweighed by the eternal weight of glory that awaited him in the City of God.

Chapter 2
Getting Leveled

*Jesus said to his disciples, "I tell you the truth,
it is hard for a rich man to enter the kingdom of
heaven."*
MATTHEW 19:23

It is very educational to watch Jesus operate in the City of Man.
The best way to describe it is to simply say that he is *not impressed.*
The glory and shame that the City of Man assigns is not a factor in
anything Jesus does. He does not receive it, he is not motivated by
it, and he does not treat people according to it. His presence in the
City of Man has a leveling effect. The valleys are lifted up and the
mountains are brought down, as Isaiah puts it. Everybody is at sea
level with Jesus. He simply ignores all the things of value in the
City of Man as if they were of no significance at all.

This point of view is something Gary Grauberger had to learn
the hard way.

Six times in his life—far more than any other prospector, including his personal hero, the famous South African miner Cecil
Rhodes—hard-driving, irreverent Gary Grauberger had found
gold. Most of the residents of Elko, the dusty mining town in east-
ern Nevada, owed their livelihoods to Gary's discoveries. Like the

legendary King Midas, Gary had the touch, and the mining company that developed his finds paid him in shares. In 1986 Gary sold his shares for fifteen million dollars. The next year he met a beautiful, twenty-two-year-old "gal" and they started living together. Gary was way up there, and as he puts it in his compact western way of speaking, "You couldn't tell me anything."[1]

Then in 1989 it seemed like somebody stopped greasing the wheels. Gary had taken some promising samples from a piece of property and, in keeping with an agreement he had with the company, had brought the find to them first. But, as Gary tells it, "We never could come to a deal, so I just said, 'To heck with it,' and decided to drill it myself."

First, he and his girlfriend got married. It was on his honeymoon that Gary first heard about the lawsuit—the company had sued him for stealing a corporate opportunity, which they later changed to a suit for fraud. Then Gary's first ex-wife sued him for more alimony just days before his new current wife announced she was filing for divorce. Shortly thereafter, another company sued, claiming he hadn't lived up to a promise to loan them money. The coup de grace came when his now second ex-wife sued him for allegedly abusing her and stealing money from her.

Gary retreated to his dream getaway in the Cayman Islands, but when he was served with a warrant, a return to the States became unavoidable. "I don't think there was anything legitimate in any of those charges or lawsuits, but I realize now that I was arrogant and hard-nosed and completely blind to how I had offended people—even people I thought were my good friends," Gary now says. "People not only wanted my money, they wanted to bring me down." His first night back in the States was spent in jail after an arrest on the abuse charges.

In 1990 the criminal charges had been dropped, but the lawsuits dragged on. Gary returned to his retreat in the Caymans for a vacation, depressed and confused about how everything could have gone from being so good to being a total disaster. One day on the beach he sat watching a man baptizing people in the surf. Afterward Gary asked the man why he was doing it and was told, "So that the dead can come to life."

"Well," Gary told him, "I'm about as dead as you can get." It wasn't long before Gary was convinced that Christ was real, and he asked to be baptized himself. From that point he began to live his life with reference to God. Underneath, however, lurked the belief that he had run up "a very favorable credit balance in [God's] ledger by allowing himself to be converted."[2]

So, when the lawsuit was settled out of court for a sum that seemed almost miraculous, Gary thought he was being rewarded by God. "I set up a company called 'Restoration Minerals' because I was convinced that—even though I was now pretty nearly broke—God was going to restore everything back to me."

Two years later Gary ground out his last cigarette with the pointed toe of his mud-caked boot. The hot Nevada sun was beating down hard on the barren desert landscape. Angry and frustrated, Gary had spent months taking ore samples on that contested piece of property that the company had signed over to him in the out-of-court settlement. So far his tests showed only a trace of gold, nothing the mining industry would call "economic." And now, to top it off, his drilling rig had broken down. Walking up a steep bluff, Gary began to scream at God out of a deep sense of injury: "Where the ——— are you God? Why have you deserted me? I thought we had a deal!"

The next thing Gary knew he was face down in the dirt, crying uncontrollably, unable to move as he sensed the awesome overwhelming presence of God. "I was terrified," Gary said. "I was finally seeing how dark I was. I felt stripped." God had shut Gary's mouth. An encounter with the Glory of the universe had filled him with loathing for his presumption and rendered him speechless.

After what seemed an eternity, Gary found he could lift his head. Looking out over the landscape, he saw something he'd never seen before during all his years in the desert. A line of fire was burning, encircling a large area of ground, even though nothing out there was combustible—just rocks and dirt. By the time he had scrambled down to the area, the fire was gone. Gary wasn't sure what it meant, but he had a humbling sense that God had spoken. He repaired his drilling rig and took a few samples from the area the fire had outlined. A few days later, the assayer's report told him he'd made his seventh strike.

THE DECEPTIVENESS OF "HAVING IT"

Gary's money had given him a sense of his own importance that was daily reinforced in the City of Man. When he walked into his bank, he expected to create a flurry of obsequious attention. Blaise Pascal lived more than three hundred years ago, but the dynamics were the same in his time. As a member of the privileged class in the France of Louis the XIV, Pascal gained shrewd insight into the City of Man: "The more promotion we seek to have on fortune's ladder takes us further from the truth, because people become increasingly more wary of offending those whose friendship is deemed most useful and see enmity as most dangerous," he wrote.[3]

In other words, success tends to create an illusion of godlikeness, and the City of Man is more than happy to fall all over itself worshiping those who have attained it. Maslow's studies uncovered this same phenomenon. The top-of-the-hierarchy subjects he identified as "self-actualized" often attracted "admirers . . . disciples and worshipers."[4] "Temper outbursts were not rare," he noted, and they "often alienated conventional people purposely."[5]

"Having it" in the City of Man tends to produce a delusional self-concept. Financial success especially creates an illusion of power, self-sufficiency, and omniscience. The glow of deity seems to cling to the successful, and the City of Man rolls out the red carpet.

JESUS IN THE CITY OF MAN

One of the glaring things you notice about Jesus is the absence of these people-pleasing tendencies. Jesus doesn't flatter or give any special deference to those on top. They are "mere men" in his eyes, and his kindness to them is usually expressed in scathing honesty.

Often his disciples wish he would show a little more deference. They are shaken by the way he calmly strips the important people of their glory. "Lord," they tell him, "you offended them."

But Jesus answers them as one who is unequivocally *not* of the City of Man: "Every plant that my heavenly Father has not planted will be pulled up by the roots" (Matt. 15:13).

It takes a lot of patient teaching on Jesus' part to get across to his disciples that "a man's life does not consist in the abundance of his possessions" (Luke 12:15). When he says "life," the idea is: value, importance, significance, identity. None of these things has anything to do with what a man has accumulated, Jesus explains. In the City of Man, these things very much determine a man's life—but not from Jesus' perspective. He is bringing in the Kingdom—the City of God—and its value system levels the hierarchy of the City of Man.

You see this not only in the people Jesus is willing to insult, but in the people he honors. The disciples try to shield him from unimportant people—like little children, for instance—but Jesus reverses their assessment. These children are the kind of people who make up the citizenship of the Kingdom, he tells them. In fact, in order to enter that kingdom, you must become like one of these.

This is the same advice Jesus gives to the rich young ruler. This fellow comes to Jesus with great weight in the City of Man. No doubt his self-concept was made up not only of his status in regard to wealth and position but his religious righteousness as well. He asks Jesus what he must do to enter the Kingdom, and after he assures Jesus that he has kept all the Commandments all his life, Jesus says, "You still lack one thing. Sell everything you have and give to the poor. . . . Then come, follow me" (Luke 18:22).

In other words: give it up. You don't get the idea that Jesus is talking about the "one more thing" the man had to add to his stature in order to deserve entrance into the City of God. He was telling him to get *rid* of all his imagined stature—his identity that was heavy with his own glory. Jesus said he was like a camel trying to get through the eye of a needle. The door to the City of God is narrow, and to enter it we must take on the identity of "merely human."

The disciples were amazed. If this man could not enter the Kingdom, then who can? Jesus tells them that God is able to do it. This is good news for all of us. God is able to break through the deceptions we unquestioningly accept. He is able to cause us to lose our illusions. Gary Grauberger's life illustrates God's ability to do this.

GETTING UNIMPRESSED

We've all seen the fish symbol on the back of cars that tells the world the occupants of the vehicle are Christians. The fish was used by the early church to symbolize Christ because the Greek word for *fish* was an acronym for "Jesus Christ, God's Son, Savior."

New York Life and
Upromise can help
you save for college!

The Company You Keep®

Join Upromise for free *today!*

This account is similar to a frequent flyer program. Simply register your credit, debit and grocery cards on Upromise's secure website and you can get college savings contributions from some of America's leading companies—such as New York Life, Kellogg's®, Coca-Cola® and ExxonMobil.*

For more information, contact us at 800-975-2436, or visit www.upromise.com/nylife.

---

*See back page for important disclosure.

Planning for college *early pays off!*

- Get a contribution* of $25-$40 when you purchase an eligible life insurance policy or other
  financial product from New York Life
  Insurance Co. and its affiliates.

- To learn more about Upromise and enroll, go
  to www.upromise.com/nylife.

For more information or if you would like to
meet with your agent or Registered
Representative about planning for you and your
family, contact us at 800-975-2436.

New York Life Insurance Company

New York Life Insurance and Annuity
Corporation (A Delaware Corporation)

51 Madison Avenue
New York, NY 10010

www.newyorklife.com

The Company You Keep®

AR02460(06/05)   SMRU 00306411CV(05/05)   3.NF-N22-01-0605

Augustine explains that the fish is an apt mystical symbol of Jesus because he was able to exist—submerged in the City of Man—and yet remain unpolluted by it.[6]

We are called to the same thing. True Christian faith, the apostle James says, means "to look after orphans and widows in their distress and to keep oneself from being polluted by the world" (James 1:27). The church he was writing to was giving special honor to the rich, and James reproved them for endorsing the hierarchy of the City of Man. Keep yourself from being polluted by that whole system, he tells them.

So how can we do it? How can we live in the City of Man without being polluted by it?

We need to get unimpressed—like Jesus.

GET UNIMPRESSED WITH STUFF

When you look at the Calvin Klein man—barefoot on the beach, with an expression that says, "I answer to no one"—what do you see? When you enter a five-star restaurant and follow the maitre d' to the linen-clad table, what do you see? When you open up *Architectural Digest* and look at the cherry paneled library with a crackling fire on the hearth, what do you see? Do you see something of great value? Something that makes great promises?

Remind yourself, "This is a lie."

We need to learn to value things with the value they will have on the Day of the Lord. Our opinions do not assign things their value. They have an actual value, an objective value, based on God's assessment of them—an assessment that will prevail on the Day of the Lord. Living unpolluted in the City of Man is very much a matter of "seeing" in the light of that day.

"In that day," Isaiah says, "men will throw away to the rodents and bats" the material things they have worshiped (Isa. 2:20). Get unimpressed *now* and you won't find yourself sold out to the incriminating evidence on the Day of the Lord.

However, do not make the mistake of thinking that the City of God and its delights are on hold until some distant future time. They are real in the present. The trouble, as Christian philosopher A. W. Tozer says, is that "the world of sense intrudes upon our attention day and night for the whole of our lifetime. It is clamourous, insistent and self-demonstrating. . . . Sin has so clouded the lenses of our hearts that we cannot see that other reality, the City of God, shining around us."[7]

The appropriate object of our affection is an unseen reality that is apprehended by the "eyes of the heart." Ask God to give you 20/20 vision so that the City of God will take on clarity and weight in your heart. "Return to Him from whom you have deeply defected, O sons of Israel," says the Lord (Isa. 31:6 NASB).

GET UNIMPRESSED WITH THE PARTY

The City of Man makes distinctions between people, and when we honor some and not others in the manner of the City of Man, we become "judges with evil thoughts" (James 2:4). We need to purify our hearts by learning to "honor all men" (1 Pet. 2:17 NASB). Paul says he now regards "no one from a worldly point of view" (2 Cor. 5:16).

Think of the City of Man as a party. Inside is the ringing of crystal, the glow of candles, laughter, a waiter passing hors d'oeuvres and drinks to beautifully dressed people engaged in animated conversation. At the door is an imposing butler. He smiles warmly and welcomes a couple who have presented him with an invitation, but his chilly dismissal sends a shabbily dressed man back into the night.

Ask the people inside what they're celebrating.

"Ourselves," they would say. "We just have a lot of joy about ourselves."

Ask God what he's going to do about this party.

"I'm going to throw a party myself," he says.

"What are you going to celebrate?" you ask.

"A wedding," he says. "We're going to celebrate that my people belong to me and that I belong to them."

"And who are you going to invite?"

"I'm inviting everyone," God says, "but most will be too busy with the business of the City of Man to pay much attention to my invitation. But the people who can't get in the world's party will be deeply honored. They will shout for joy. And, ultimately, those who refused my invitation will find themselves on the outside looking in."

This is not fiction. This is how God's Word tells us it really is. Furthermore, God tells *us* to invite the people on the outside to *our* party. Invite the boring people. The people with no party of their own. Invite the ones with nothing to put on the table. The people the City of Man doesn't see—*you* see them. *You* be interested in them. *You* treat them with honor.

How can we care about these people when we are so conditioned to seeing people in reference to ourselves? Are they relevant to our arena or the arena we might want to get into? What can they do for us? Can they add to our glory or be an audience for it? If not, then they practically don't exist.

God gives us the solution to our problem. He tells us that the lightweights in the City of Man are *his* special concern. If you are sitting on an airplane next to a nondescript young woman, you might hardly notice her as you busily put the final touches on your résumé. But if you glance at the tag on her bag and realize she is the daughter of the man with whom you're going to interview for a job, she will suddenly become very interesting to you. Ask God to give you *his* eyes to see people as *he* sees them so that they'll take on weight in your estimation. He says that everything you do for one of these will be seen and rewarded by him.

GET UNIMPRESSED WITH YOURSELF

That's really the bottom-line challenge—because we seem to be addicted to our own glory.

Gary Grauberger was deeply impressed with himself when he was rolling in money. Even when bankruptcy threatened, he still adopted the self-satisfaction of thinking himself a pretty good guy. When God leveled him in the desert, however, Gary genuinely despised himself—he saw himself as something very small compared to God, and his boasting mouth was shut. But, as Gary tells it, in a few months—he had recovered.

The strike Gary made was phenomenal. It yielded two million ounces of gold and fifteen million ounces of silver, and when he sold his part in 1998, he had thirty-eight million dollars. Gary had gotten the message loud and clear that this ore was "discovered" by God and that—in his use of it—he was answerable to God. So, he started giving it away. Pretty soon, however, "I thought I was doing the Lord some pretty big favors," Gary says.

One night Gary went to hear a speaker at a local church. It was not an impressive meeting. Only about thirty people were scattered among the chairs in the meeting hall, and the public address system wasn't working. Up front stood an unimposing visiting speaker from the Philippines—dressed in a threadbare suit and with holes in his shoes. When the man began speaking, Gary could barely hear him. "I stand here in fear and trembling as I preach the Word of God," the speaker said. As he proceeded, however, his words began to ring with authority.

"He asked us if we were doing things to please men or to please God," Gary remembers, "and he nailed every one of us, especially me. He said we were defiling the church with our pride. All of us were either crying or staring at the floor. But instead of leaving us feeling bad, he started telling us that's the reason Christ was crucified. I was crying my head off."

THE LEVELING EFFECT OF THE CROSS

Although Gary had been able to recover from the fear of God, he hasn't recovered yet from the fearful love of God. The apostle Paul said, "May I never boast except in the cross of our Lord Jesus Christ, through which the world has been crucified to me, and I to the world" (Gal. 6:14). The cross renders the glory/shame struggle of the City of Man obsolete by showing us the repugnance of our boasting. It levels us with an unequivocal revelation of the "lowness" of the place we deserve and makes us despise the things that led us to boast. Yet at the same time, it breaks our hearts by revealing the depths to which the Son of God was willing to descend in order to rescue us from the City of Man and make us his own.

It's in the cross that we understand the dynamics of the City of God. Boasting is excluded for everyone except Christ Jesus. He alone is exalted. But we are exalted *in him*. "God raised us up with Christ and seated us with him in the heavenly realms" (Eph. 2:6). Everything that is his—righteousness, life, wisdom, the glory of the sons and daughters of God—are given to us *in him*. This is why glory is not competitive in the City of God. All the distinctions have been eliminated because "Christ is all and is in all" (Col. 3:11).

The Scottish preacher Alistair Begg says he carries a little card with him into the pulpit that says, "I renounce my desire for human praise, for the approval of my peers, the need for public recognition. I deliberately put these aside today, content to hear you whisper, 'Well done, my faithful servant.'" He looks at it whenever he is tempted to take a "wee bit" of glory for himself. "It's worn out," he says. "I've had to replace it several times because I can't do it."

No, we can't do it. But the gospel can.

Chapter 3
Learning to See

*"Stop judging by mere appearances,
and make a right judgment."*
JESUS TO THE PHARISEES, JOHN 7:24

What are the real power centers in the City of Man? Are there smoky back rooms where the real players move the chess pieces and then decide what public spin to put on things? Are governments the true seats of power where money can be exacted from us and laws made that govern us? What about Wall Street? Allen Greenspan?

Who really runs the world?

C. Everett Koop figured the science of medicine was a power center with clear potential for real good. Early in life Koop decided to use his mind and his hands to heal. A high achiever with a focused goal, he became a courageous crusader for children in the field of pediatrics—and eventually the best-known surgeon general in the history of the United States.

It was during his early years at Children's Hospital in Philadelphia when Koop first began to ask questions. Was there a spiritual realm operating in harmony with the medical science he practiced every day? Were the intense pain and suffering of his young patients and their parents just tragically arbitrary events?

Even of his detractors, few would deny Koop's brilliance. His pediatric bow tie and Lincolnesque beard give the first clues—Koop operates with a unique disregard for the pressure of other people's opinions. He pioneered changes that revolutionized the practice of pediatric surgery around the world—never hesitating to shake up the status quo.

Koop's strong personality was demonstrated early in his career when he once arranged to appear before a conference of physicians to challenge the diagnosis of Dr. Milton Rappaport, a senior doctor. "The day came," Koop says. "Rap presented the case as a simple one of empyema. . . . Then it was my turn. . . . Rap, the 'good ole boy,' erudite, knowledgeable, the house officer's role model, fount of all knowledge, weighed in at more than three hundred pounds. I, the young upstart, unproven disrupter of limited horizons . . . weighed in at a mere two hundred pounds."[1]

Koop not only convinced the jury of his peers, he saved the day. He made an indisputable case that the procedure Dr. Rappaport was recommending would probably result in death for the young patient. If doctors are allowed their god-complexes, then Koop qualified for a god-of-gods complex.

And yet . . . his failures left him deeply aware of his own powerlessness.

THE CURTAIN OPENS

In his best-selling book *Why Do Bad Things Happen to Good People?*, Rabbi Harold Kushner concludes that God, himself, is powerless to intervene.

"Nonsense!" Koop would say.

"Even before I became a Christian, it seemed to me that if God weren't sovereign, then there's no point in having a god. If someone can thwart God's sovereign plan, then he can't be much of a god," Koop says emphatically.[2]

"I have found that everyone, regardless of their beliefs, needs to know that someone is in control when bad things happen. They want to know that the things affecting their lives are not just random and out of control." Koop wanted to know that too.

Koop's valued friend and assisting nurse at Children's Hospital, Erna Goulding, saw his struggle for answers and suggested he listen to Reverend Donald Gray Barnhouse at Tenth Presbyterian Church in center-city Philadelphia. The next Sunday Koop slipped in the back door. Hearing Dr. Barnhouse awakened something in Koop. The curtain started to draw back to reveal the unseen reality.

"I came to realize that my life wasn't just a series of dilemmas, followed by happy coincidences," Koop says.[3]

He understood that suffering entered the world because of the justice of God upon the sin of humankind—that it is an indictment of the City of Man, not of God.

Yet he also saw that suffering is encompassed within the purposes of God's mercy and that God has provided ultimate answers through the death and resurrection of his Son.

Koop realized that his own life and all the opportunities he'd been given were planned by God for his purposes. In fact, not a molecule moves, not a sparrow falls from the sky except by the will of God. God does not act randomly.

Within a few months, Koop had put his faith in Christ. "I was a believer. . . . I acknowledged the Lord Jesus Christ in my life and rested my abiding faith in the sovereignty of God."[4]

After that, things were different. When he operated on a small child's body, whether the procedure was as simple as repairing a hernia or as life-threatening as correcting a serious congenital defect, a newfound humility prompted him to entrust his hands into the hands of the Source of all healing. When medicine failed, he was comforted profoundly by his faith that God was in control.

THE REAL POWER CENTER

What Koop thought was a power center in the City of Man was actually controlled by God. This is true of every apparent center of power in the City of Man. Governments are established by God to maintain order and administer justice. Yet the government's potential to do good is limited. When Koop became surgeon general, he applied his influence so every cigarette package carried the warning, "The surgeon general has determined that cigarette smoking is dangerous to your health," yet his seemingly powerful office had no power to break addiction.

When governments are doing whatever limited good they've been established by God to do, it's because God is doing good through them. Yet, even when they are very bad, they are under God's control. "[God] is sovereign over the kingdoms of men" (Dan. 4:25), Nebuchadnezzar was forced to admit. "He does as he pleases / with the powers of heaven / and the peoples of the earth. / No one can hold back his hand / or say to him: 'What have you done?'" (Dan. 4:35).

The truth is—whatever plans the City of Man may have, God has an overruling plan. His purpose prevails (see Prov. 19:21). Pilate thought he was in the power seat. After all, he represented Caesar, the greatest ruler of the most glorious kingdom the City of Man had yet to see. "Don't you realize I have power either to free you or to crucify you?" Pilate asked Jesus (John 19:10). But Jesus responded that Pilate's power was only granted to him by God. God is the real power center. He "brings death and makes alive; / he brings down to the grave and raises up. / The LORD sends poverty and wealth; / he humbles and he exalts" (1 Sam. 2:6–7).

God is in control. He has a plan, and he's seeing it fulfilled.

The power centers are just part of the backdrop. The real action is going on somewhere else. The chief issues in life, as Augustine insists, are not related to the City of Man but to the City of God. The meaning of history is not to be found in the apparent power moves within the City of Man, but in the hidden drama of God's unfolding plan.

THE HIDDEN DRAMA

As a teenager, Joni Eareckson Tada had already committed herself to God. The youngest of four girls, she was attractive, popular, athletic, and the captain of her high school lacrosse team. Life held all kinds of promise.

But in 1967, at the age of seventeen, Joni was involved in an accident that radically changed her life and her understanding of how God works. Two months before starting college, Joni and her sister were swimming in the Chesapeake Bay. It was late afternoon, and the surface of the water reflected the setting sun. At the edge of a raft, Joni sprang up in an athletic dive and broke the water's surface with her arms. But instead of gliding through the water, she struck a rock, shattering her spine. Her sister was able to pull Joni out of the water and call for help. Joni was taken to the hospital. Weeks passed before she was told that she would be a quadriplegic for the rest of her life.

Joni was thunderstruck. Her life reeled. Then she was darkly, savagely angry. Immobilized by both paralysis and despair, she lay violently moving her head back and forth trying to break her neck higher up so she could die.

Eventually Joni was forced to acknowledge that there was no escape. She couldn't die, yet she didn't know how to live. Hazel, a black nurse's aid from Mississippi, was feeding her dinner one evening when Joni let the half-chewed food dribble out of her mouth. Hazel slammed down the fork and told her, "You get yourself together, girl."[5]

After Hazel left, Joni choked out a prayer. "I can't live like this. Please help me." She began moving in the direction of God, and answers—slowly, quietly—moved into her heart. If God chose this for her, then it came from the hand of her all-wise Father who loved her so much he gave his Son for her. He must have taken into account all the consequences—the humiliations and the frustrations. It must be OK. Joni was able, eventually, to receive her paralysis as being from his hand, and this acquiescence brought her a kind of exultant joy.

"We gloriously gain when we kiss shattered dreams good-bye," she explains. "We forfeit earthly pleasure but rise to the euphoria that is out of this world."[6]

Koop and his wife, Betty, suffered the death of one of their children a few years after they became Christians. Koop had had a premonition in January of that year. He realized that five of the specialists at Children's Hospital had children with the very same defect or disease as their specialty. Surprisingly, these afflictions hadn't led to their choices of specialties—they came afterward! With trepidation Koop considered what his specialty might be. After a presentation to a medical school class that later became an article in *Reader's Digest,* it dawned on him that he had become an expert on counseling parents of dying children. He also became convinced that he would lose a child to death.

Within the year, his third son, David, a junior at Dartmouth, died in a rock-climbing accident.

When the news of David's death came, the first thing the family did was gather in a circle to pray. Koop asked that the Lord, "having taken David from us according to his perfect will, would please show us some of the things he would accomplish through David's death."[7]

The Koops wrote a book about this experience but didn't publish it for several years. "Our other kids said it made us sound too special to God," Koop explains. "Well, I never felt so special in my life. I felt like I was lifted right into the Godhead."

Like Joni, the Koops experienced a triumphal joy in the midst of excruciating pain. In the estimation of the City of Man, these believers suffered huge and meaningless losses. But as citizens of the City of God, they saw an unseen reality that far outweighed their suffering. They were center stage in the hidden drama, and as they acknowledged God's rule and embraced his love, there was a great victory. God was glorified by his people in the midst of the City of Man.

OVERCOMING THE WORLD

God's purpose is not to progressively improve the City of Man. That city will be thriving and going about its business when the Judgment comes. Still, in the midst of the City of Man, God is triumphing in and through the faith of his people. That's his plan. That's the hidden drama. Whenever a citizen of the City of God responds—not to the visible appearance of things but to the unseen reality behind the scenes—God is glorified.

Satan is a significant player in this drama. His influence is largely hidden, but Scripture calls him "the ruler of this world" (John 12:31 NASB). He was the behind-the-scenes plotter of the rebellion that spawned the City of Man. His strategy from the beginning has been to mislead humanity into disobedience to God through lies and false appearances.

The hidden drama of history is a battle God has chosen to wage against this enemy and the city he rules—a battle the Son of God has already won. Jesus refused the glory of the City of Man when Satan offered it to him in the wilderness. Later, as he considered whether he would ask his Father to rescue him from the cross, Jesus made it clear that he was resolved to accomplish the final victory in this battle. "What shall I say?" he asked. "'Father, save me from this hour'? No, it was for this very reason I came to this hour." And then he added, "Father, glorify your name!" (John 12:27–28).

Jesus understood the hidden drama. He knew the central role was his. He told his disciples, "Now is the time for judgment on this world; now the prince of this world will be driven out" (John 12:31). But we have a role to play as well. Jesus was the author and finisher of our faith. We follow his lead, and whenever we live by faith rather than by sight, God's name is glorified and Satan is "dissed" (as the kids say), and we get a taste of exultant victory that sustains us even in sorrow.

This battle drama is taking place on the stage of the City of Man, which has been the domain of God's enemies, the arena where Satan has flaunted his destructive successes. The battle is hot and the pressures are great. We are on center stage surrounded by a crowd of unseen witnesses. When faith is victorious, the heavens rejoice. As 1 John 5:4 says, "This is the victory that has overcome the world, even our faith." There are two weapons our faith employs in this battle—"the blood of the Lamb" and "the word of [our] testimony" (Rev. 12:11).

OVERCOMING BY THE BLOOD OF THE LAMB

The blood of the Lamb is the gospel. When Jesus was raised from the dead, God enthroned him at his right hand and gave him the whole world as his inheritance. The gospel is God's testimony that Jesus is his anointed King who will execute judgment on the City of Man that rejected him and put him to death.

"'Why do the nations rage . . . in vain? . . . against the Lord and against his Anointed One," the Jerusalem church prayed in Acts 4:25–26. They were seeing the antagonism of the City of Man toward the lordship of the Son of God firsthand. The world hates the gospel because it hates the lordship of Christ that the gospel declares.

And it hates the judgment it implies.

"Jesus crucified" lays the ax to the City of Man. It's the first shudder from the blows of God's judgment that will come upon the sin of the world. But while the gospel may warn of judgment, it offers the exact opposite of judgment. The gospel is a message from God to the world that says: "Look! The judgment is laid upon the Son of God instead of you! Look at the blood of the Lamb and repent and believe and be forgiven for your sins."

When we believe the gospel, we break ranks with the City of Man and run for refuge to the City of God. For any hard-hearted, self-glorifying citizen of the world to humbly repent before the cross is nothing short of a miracle. It is a miracle that gives evidence that God is able to prevail over the City of Man—not only in judgment, but by claiming its citizens as his own. In the initial believing of the gospel comes a transformation from self-will to submission to God.

The power of the gospel doesn't stop there. Paul says the gospel *continues* to grow and bear fruit in us (Col. 1:6). We don't progress beyond the gospel but, as James says, the gospel becomes like a mirror where we continually gaze upon our natural selves. The sight is profoundly humbling, but the deeper we're humbled, the deeper the gospel gets. We see it widen and deepen like the spring of water in Ezekiel's vision of the City of God. First it's a trickle. Then it's up to our knees. Pretty soon we can't touch bottom. The "blood of the Lamb"—grace poured out for sinners—is an ocean.

As our vision improves, we realize: "I can't see beyond the love of Christ Jesus for me. It stretches in every direction further than the eye of my heart can see." This kind of faith will overcome anything life has to offer—be it the appeal of City-of-Man glory or the devastation of paralysis or the death of a dearly loved son.

OVERCOMING BY THE WORD OF TESTIMONY

The word of testimony moves us beyond the arena of the heart into the arena of action, where faith is lived out against great resistance. When Pilate looked at Jesus—scourged, dripping with spit, crowned with thorns—and asked, with a bit of incredulity, "Are you a king?" and Jesus answered, "It is as you have said"— there was a great triumph. It was just one of many on the road to the cross.

"Faith is being sure of what we hope for and certain of what we do not see" (Heb. 11:1). Jesus spoke confidently of unseen things knowing that Pilate not only couldn't see any evidence of Jesus' kingship but that he was cynical about the whole idea. Jesus gave testimony to the things not seen in the midst of a hostile and unbelieving world.

OVERCOMING THE SPELL

Pilate epitomized the sophistication of the City of Man, which treats religion as something irrelevant for everyone except children and old women. He was pragmatic. He was a man of the world. He knew how things worked, so he didn't want to hear talk about unseen things. When Revelation 18:23 speaks about the final judgment on the City of Man, it says, "By your magic spell all the nations were led astray." We take part in the victory over the City of Man when we refuse to succumb to that spell and, instead, give testimony to the unseen reality.

The spell *is* powerful. The City of Man goes about its business with an implacable disregard for Christ. Go inside a skyscraper in the business district of any metropolis. Look at the glass and polished brass. Watch the self-important bustle of people going about their business. The seen things seem to mock the reality of the unseen things. They cast a spell that says, "I am all there is."

Faith has to cut against the grain in order to triumph. It must lay hold of the unseen realities and live them out in the face of the opposition of the City of Man. That's what the Bible means by *perseverance*. There is great resistance to our faith—within and without.

Overcoming is the battle of faith to resist the assault of unbelief that permeates the City of Man. We must struggle to be unashamed of the gospel in an environment that views it with contempt. More than once we're forced to learn to fear God, not man. When the world says "fool" we must learn to say "so be it" and bear the name of Christ with joy. When finally death intrudes, faith must look it in the eye and ask, "Grave, where is your triumph?"

When we resolve to live for the private praise of the Father rather than public approval of others, we will inevitably feel the undertow of the world. Overcoming takes practice and daily repentance. We must learn to see that our gains and loses in the City of Man aren't as desperately important as they seem. This becomes possible as we learn to see that Jesus is our portion and our glorious inheritance. Sometimes it takes pain to break the spell the City of Man has cast on us and to get our feet moving down the road to the City of God.

But Jesus gives us *his* faith, and so we overcome. His redemption triumphs, and the courts of heaven resound with exultant joy.

Even when the City of Man is at its worst and persecutes Christians for their faith, the victory still goes to the City of God.

The greatest triumph of faith comes when believers, like Jesus, "love not their lives even unto death" (Rev. 12:11 RSV). The martyrs have left their testimonies: obedient submission to the Lord who died for us, especially when it's painful, is victory and exquisite joy.

While our little martyrdoms may be less costly than death, they do not go unnoticed by the crowd of witnesses. Take for instance, a twenty-two-year-old atheist—a woman of Jewish heritage—who finished the Book of John and closed the Bible. "This has the ring of truth," she marveled. "I believe it." Two months later, wealthy Uncle Levi heard about her conversion and wrote her out of his will.

"Leap for joy!" Jesus says.

Remember: the City of Man's judgment is 180 degrees off. You are part of the hidden drama. Faith overcomes the world. Redemption triumphs in the midst of the City of Man.

Peter says the testing of our faith through trials will result in "praise, glory and honor when Jesus Christ is revealed" (1 Pet. 1:7). On that day, the hidden drama of history won't be hidden anymore. All the stories will be told. Even the victories of faith previously seen only by the unseen cloud of witnesses will be recounted with joy. The glory of our tried and tested faith will adorn the City of God. Our "righteous acts" that have been "washed in the blood of the Lamb" will beautify the bride of Christ (see Rev. 19:7–8). It will be a glorious party—the wedding feast of the Lamb.

SEEING THE UNSEEN REALITY

Jesus perused the rabble gathered around him—the irritable, disheartened, greedy, deceptive, self-promoting citizens of the City of Man—and told his disciples, "Open your eyes and look at the fields. They are white for harvest." His vision was 20/20. Jesus was never deceived by mere appearances. He looked at humanity and saw a vast multitude from every nation who would be sovereignly drawn into the City of God. He saw people he loved so much that he was willing to lay down his life to rescue them from their lostness.

SEEING THE WORLD

Jesus is calling us to open the eyes of our hearts and learn to see the potential that he sees—to see the City of Man as not only a rebellious place ripe for judgment but as a field ripe for harvest. When the disciples asked Jesus if they should bring down judgment on a less-than-welcoming Samaritan city, Jesus told them that they hadn't quite caught the spirit of the thing. God is issuing an invitation to the citizens of the City of God through the gospel: "Escape the wrath. Come to the party." Have no doubt—the banquet hall will be filled.

Holding on to the Good News in the face of opposition is certainly a triumph of faith, but seeing that the unseen King is drawing the nations to himself and participating in that endeavor is an even greater triumph of faith. Food for the hungry, justice for the oppressed, compassion for the hurting—these are all foretastes of the City of God and testimonies to its reality. We are called to halt our headlong pursuit of our City-of-Man goals and offer these things to the needy world. However, when we offer the *gospel*, we do more. We open the door so the hurting can come in and take up permanent residence at the banquet table.

Unbelief within ourselves and in the City of Man puts up a formidable resistance. It's natural for us to see things the way the City of Man sees them. Faith shrivels at the thought. That's why the church in Jerusalem prayed for Spirit-given boldness. Boldness comes from being certain of things not seen.

When C. Everett Koop's phone rings, it may be the President or a member of Congress seeking out his advice.

Even in retirement his campaign against tobacco continues un-abated, and if he spots you smoking, be prepared for a one-on-one lecture. When asked why he thinks God placed him in a position of prominence, Koop says, "It gives me a platform in the world to testify to Christ."

One week after his son's death, Koop was scheduled to speak to a large men's group. Rather than cancel, he spoke to them about his hope of eternal life for David and the peace he had in the face of this death. His suffering gave credibility to his testimony.

Not long after Joni was paralyzed she began to speak about the sympathizing love of Jesus. A fireman whose hands had been burned off challenged her: "Big deal. What good does it do me?"

"I don't have all the answers," she said, "but I would rather be in this wheelchair knowing Jesus than on my feet without him."

Joni has experienced the compassion of God.

"God, like a father, doesn't just give advice," she writes. "He gives himself. He becomes the husband to the grieving widow . . . the comforter to the barren woman . . . the father of the orphaned."[8]

Joni's work on behalf of the handicapped is a testimony to the compassion of God. It doesn't provide ultimate solutions, but it points the way to the City of God—where there will be the great and final wiping away of tears.

SEEING EACH OTHER

"Patrick" is the president of a nonprofit trust that distributes millions of dollars in grants every year. On Sunday, Pat and his wife, "Linda," worship in a school building with a handful of other believers.[9] Theirs are the only white faces in the congregation, and their income is beyond the comprehension of the other members.

Pat explains why he and Linda worship there: "We are blessed when we are around poor Christians. They love us so much and we love them. We bless each other." Pat first realized this dynamic when he was on a fact-finding trip to Uganda and met African Christians whose lives were radically different from his own.

"We're so afraid of being poor. Where the Scripture says, 'If we have food and drink we will be content,' that just doesn't make sense to us. Yet when you get around poor Christians, you realize that poverty isn't such a terrible thing. It takes away your fear. There is so much beauty and joy in their lives. We need to see that so we can realize that money isn't nearly as significant as we think it is."

There is nothing patronizing about what Pat is saying. Yes, he and Linda have helped significantly with the financial needs of the other church members, but the need for each other is mutual. Pat and Linda *need* to be in fellowship with Christians who are low on the scale in the City of Man. They *need* to see how Christ prevails in those circumstances and to be humbled by it.

But there is another reason why there is such a unique joy—such a blessing—when rich and poor worship together. The apostle James writes to a church consisting of both rich and poor. "The brother in humble circumstances ought to take pride in his high position. But the one who is rich should take pride in his low position, because he will pass away like a wild flower" (James 1:9–11). James is saying that the poor Christian should reject the judgment of the City of Man and have a triumphant joy because of his high position as a son and heir in the City of God. The wealthy Christian does the same thing—he exultantly rejects the judgment of the City of Man that says he is superior to the poor man.

When rich and poor Christians have fellowship, the City of Man's hierarchy is leveled. Together they give a hearty embrace to the invisible reality. God's redemption prevails even to the extent of overcoming hostility between people.

"Look and be radiant, / your heart will throb and swell with joy; . . . to you the riches of the nations will come," Isaiah 60:5 tells the City of God. Not only does Christ possess us, but we possess each other. We don't compete. We exult over each other the way a man gets a charge when he looks at his new sports car and says, "This baby is all mine!"

The glory of all the nations is flowing into the City of God and adorning it. People everywhere are coming to Christ. Competition is being replaced by mutual possession. That's why Pat and Linda and the other members of their church can take such great delight in one another. They look at each other and see a multifaceted treasure, and they exult.

Exultation is all about victory. It's like the touchdown dance pro-football players perform in the end zone. It's Jesus—the author and finisher of our faith—leading us in triumphal procession to the City of God.

Chapter 4
Leaning Hard

"Apart from me you can do nothing."
JESUS TO HIS DISCIPLES, JOHN 15:5B

Confidence.

Do you wonder what it would be like to have it?

Many of us feel as if we missed the meeting when life was explained. The world for us is an intimidating place full of people who seem to know something we don't know.

What would it be like to wake up feeling like a racehorse pawing the ground at the starting gate? To see the world as an arena designed to test our mettle—and to actually relish the challenge? Not a bluff. Not the kind of confidence you pump up from reading positive-thinking success books, but something innate.

Studies show that confidence is a key characteristic of the great American hero—the entrepreneur. Bill Gates may not look like a hero, and no one who heard his testimony at the antitrust hearings would say he sounds like a hero, but he has executed a perfect run in an extreme sport. Neither climbing the corporate ladder nor inheriting big bucks appeals to our imagination as does the entrepreneur because his success is not contingent. He's an independent operator—alone against the odds.

Harvard Medical School psychologist Dr. Steven Berglas refers to it in a column entitled "Entrepreneurial Ego." He says that entrepreneurs are often "headstrong control freaks (in a laissez-faire way) who march to a very different drummer."[1] "Control freak" may be a little strong. Reluctant to relinquish their autonomy, certainly.

Doug Cobb had an entrepreneurial streak that was like an itch he had to scratch. It made him impatient to think about working an eight-to-five job for someone else at a set salary. He had an unquestioned confidence in himself, an unflagging optimism that made him a natural risk-taker, and an intuitive sense about the marketplace. Plus he was a very hard worker.

In the early 1980s Bill Gates was between Harvard and Microsoft, and Steve Jobs was just releasing the Apple IIe computer. Doug wanted an idea that would give him a cut of the impending personal computer boom but wouldn't require a big investment of capital—which he didn't have. Reasoning that the PC would soon become a nonnegotiable necessity—and that most businesses had practically no expertise in using software—Doug started a newsletter and called it *The Cobb Report*. Adopting a case-study method, he provided an easy-to-understand explanation of the software available and how it applied to specific tasks. Software companies were more than happy to include information about his publication in their retail packages, and the newsletter quickly became required reading for many computer users.

In an astonishingly short time, the Cobb newsletter was in demand all over the country. As the computer industry exploded and the computer options for businesses became more confusing, *The Cobb Report* mutated into specialty editions with applications for the Macintosh and IBM worlds. Instead of selling one, Doug would sell anyone two or three. Practically overnight he created a market and owned it.

Then he sold it, for a bundle, and started a venture capital company. Success again.

"I've never been content to stay at one level of success," Cobb explains. "It's fun while you're working it—but once it's a done deal, it starts to get boring. Then it's time to move on to the next challenge."[2]

Unfortunately, when "luck" seems to be smiling on us, unseen spiritual dangers often lurk beneath the surface. Cobb, a Christian, says the reason for that is no mystery: "Success blinds you to your true spiritual condition. People think you're wonderful. You don't have material needs. You can buy security and comfort. You give yourself credit for the things you've accomplished. You say to yourself, 'What needs can I possibly have that God can fulfill for me?'"

Even as a believer it's easy to drift into self-confident independence. It becomes a habit to be always the benefactor, never the supplicant. As one pastor says, tongue in cheek, "It's hard not to feel superior when you really *are* superior."

Doug had all his sails unfurled and was tacking to the wind when he entered his latest endeavor. This time he moved into the public sector and took on the CEO role for Greater Louisville, Inc.—a chamber of commerce economic development agency set up to attract and support entrepreneurship for the city of Louisville. He began applying his previously successful techniques to this new challenge. Unfortunately, Doug had a blind side, and he was about to get blindsided in a big way.

"Greater Louisville, Inc., has historically been very 'white' and very big-business dominated," Doug explains. "My politics on racial issues have been pretty conservative, and that has led me to a certain point of view. My understanding and my compassion for black people was really lacking. I had no idea how divided we were racially here in Louisville and as a country. I had a whole bunch of obliviousness."

Doug suddenly found himself under heavy public attack for racial insensitivity. He needed help.

Tourists going to upper Egypt to view the remains of the great temple of Luxor see a strange sight. At the top of one of the soaring columns is a small house. A local farmer built his home on what he thought was bedrock. But then the archaeologists arrived. By the time their excavations were complete, the farmer's house was nearly eighty feet in the air.[3]

Life is often like that. We operate with blind confidence in our own abilities and resources until we suddenly find we're eighty feet up and needing help desperately.

"Things suddenly got scary," Doug says. "I ran up against the limit of my abilities. I was facing something that was beyond my capacity. It's been like that for the last two years in this job. I've been out on the edge, with no delusions that I can get the job done. This has been the biggest development of my life—because it has diminished my self-reliance and increased my reliance on God."

But, wait a minute. What happened to Doug's confidence? Isn't confidence a good thing?

The problem isn't confidence. It's *misplaced* confidence that gets us into trouble. Confidence in our own strength, our own power to get things done, our own judgment—this kind of confidence can motivate us out from under the covers when the alarm goes off. It may even carry us pretty far in life. What's more, it's highly recommended by the City of Man. Eventually, however, it will prove to have been a mistake.

THE TWO HUMANITIES

The citizens of the two cities—the City of Man and the City of God—are diametrically opposed on this issue of confidence. It's one of the ways you can tell them apart.

Cain was condemned to wander the earth after he murdered his brother. A wanderer can never stockpile security. He can never cultivate his own sustenance. He lives an insecure life. Yet Cain didn't remain a wanderer. Instead, he built a city where people co-operated in a mutual endeavor to provide for themselves. Their goal was a self-sufficient—rather than a God-sufficient—society.

The drive behind all the hustle and bustle of the City of Man—then and now—is an unquestioned confidence that "we can do it." We can fend for ourselves. We can gain life. This is seen in the muscle flexing of Cain's offspring, Lamech. He boasted that he could take care of himself, and if anybody messed with him, they would get back seven times what they dished out. The City of Man does not look too kindly on weakness.

In contrast, the citizens of the City of God know their need. They have no illusions about their ultimate inadequacy to provide for themselves. Seth named his first child "Enosh," which meant "frailty"—in other words "not strong, not in control." That sounds pretty strange. Why would anyone want to label a baby with the declaration that he is weak?

Seth knew that the prerequisite for putting confidence in God is to disclaim any confidence in ourselves. Doug Cobb had to learn that principle. While he could have given a well-articulated, biblically based theology of trusting God, it took learning to distrust himself—giving up on the confidence he had in his own abilities—to teach him to look to God.

"Dependence on God for salvation and for all other things besides" characterized the godly line, says Dr. James Boice in his book, *Two Cities, Two Loves.* "The godly knew they were not self-sufficient. So they threw themselves on God."[4]

Notice the order—they first recognized that they were not sufficient in themselves. Then, in that knowledge, they turned their eyes away from themselves and looked to God.

REGARDING THE WORK OF THE LORD

The wicked, according to the psalmist David, "show no regard for the works of the LORD and what his hands have done" (Ps. 28:5).

The problem with the wicked—who are just common everyday citizens of the City of Man—is that they do not look to the work of God's hand. They are too preoccupied with the work of their own hands: "Look what I have accomplished. Look what I have accumulated. Look what I plan to do in the future."

Jesus warns that this kind of misplaced confidence can take us right through to the end of our lives—when we will be in for a big shock. The work of our own hands is ultimately not going to be sufficient.

It may seem as though confidence in ourselves *plus* ability *plus* getting the breaks *equals* accomplishment. But the apostle James says that even entrepreneurs shouldn't assume they have any kind of autonomous power to make things work: "Listen, you who say, 'Today or tomorrow we will go to this or that city, spend a year there, carry on business and make money.' Why, you do not even know what will happen tomorrow. What is your life? You are a mist that appears for a little while and then vanishes. Instead, you ought to say, 'If it is the Lord's will, we will live and do this or that'" (James 4:13–15).

Success. God allows it. God can frustrate it. Regardless, we cannot ultimately sustain our own lives by it. We are "frailty." We die.

Nonetheless, this rather obvious inevitability doesn't sink in with us. When death actually happens, it comes as something of a surprise. In the meantime we keep on planning and striving in pursuit of the illusion of having a secure and independent life. It is when we reach the end of our self-sufficiency that we become disillusioned in a good way. We realize we're not competent to provide for ourselves.

That's when our attention can be redirected—away from ourselves and onto the work of the Lord's hand. When we learn to call ourselves "frailty," we get in touch with reality. This will save us a lot of misspent effort. We can stop messing around in the futility of our own efforts and go directly to the one who can really get the job done.

Doug Cobb is going through this process. "I'm learning to continually focus on him and to depend on his power to get things done," Doug says.

It hasn't been easy. When things started falling apart, Doug's first reaction was to get out. "When this racial issue came up, it was all over the papers. It was very frustrating and humiliating," he recalls. "Even now it is the one thing people remember, and it's really discouraging. I wanted to quit. I thought, *Who needs this? Why should I fool with this?* But God made it vividly clear through an answer to prayer that this is specifically what he wants me to do."

Doug now spends a lot of time in prayer. "One of the things I pray is 'Lord, it's really hard for me to do this when I don't want to.' The pattern in my life has been that I do what I want. That's been successful for me—doing the things I really love—having that energy. Now, every day I ask God to show me his hand in this—to give me a little encouragement. And he has. I've made contact with some people of faith in the black community. We share a commitment to Christ, so we have something to start with—something to build on."

THE CITY BUILT ON STRENGTH

Unfortunately, the City of Man is not a place where we can easily expose our weaknesses. While the City of Man smiles on the sleek, the put-together, the confident, and the strong; it can turn its back overnight. The smiles will turn into frowns of disapproval. As Doug found out, the world can go from being the oyster that nestles your pearl, to an uncomfortable place of cold, unsympathetic judgment.

Cecilia Chacon's story is a little different from Doug's.[5] On moving day Cecilia's energy was boundless. She chattered away as each piece was unloaded from the moving van, gesturing expansively as she explained just where to place it in the new house, her flamboyant personality overflowing with excitement. She had come a long way from the mobile home park where her mother's alcoholism and her father's desertion meant she and her siblings had to fend for themselves. Her husband, Daniel, an immigrant from Chile who initially could only find work as a night watchman, had "made good" by sheer hard work and frugality. He was now in charge of maintaining the large estate of the head of a Fortune 500 company—a job that involved supervising a massive staff as well as personally chauffeuring the boss. Cecilia and Daniel shared a dream—to escape being outcasts and to never let their own children feel the indignity they have endured.

Fast forward one year and we'll find a very different Cecilia. It slowly became apparent that being able to afford the upscale neighborhood didn't mean being accepted by the upscale neighbors. Cool reserve met every overture of friendship Cecilia offered. She noticed that she and Daniel were the only ones in their neighborhood who worked up a sweat maintaining their own residence. The neighbors seemed to look through them as if they didn't exist.

Cecilia responded on two levels. She drew a circle around herself and her little family and started making angry judgments of her own: "These people have never worked hard a day in their lives. If they hadn't been born with advantages, they could never have pulled themselves up like we have." At the same time, Cecilia's childhood insecurities emerged again. She asked Daniel to mow the lawn early in the morning before the neighbors came out to get their papers. It became very important that her children never look bad, either on the Little League field or in their performance at school.

The City of Man is not a very friendly place. Its ever-assessing attitude creates fear and isolation. We instinctively realize it is ill-advised to expose our weaknesses in hopes of receiving mercy from the City of Man. Instead, we choose either to respond with hardened, self-protective judging in kind, or we make an all-consuming effort to gain the world's approval. If we lack the self-confidence to do battle, we may become crippled, if not immobilized, by anxiety.

Like Lamech at the beginning of biblical history, Friedrich Nietzsche also epitomized the City of Man's contempt for weakness. He scorned Christianity as a religion of the weak. He said "the well-constituted and dominant . . . the gifted, learned, spiritually independent . . . the well-constituted, the masterful" were not exalted by the Christian faith. Instead, he said, it "appeals to the disinherited."[6]

Nietzsche was right about that. God is angry with the City of Man for exalting its strength and independence and for oppressing the weak. He has responded by sending his Son to identify with the "disinherited," and he insists that anyone who wishes to be among his people must take the place of admitted weakness and look to him alone for hope and help.

This attitude doesn't go down well in the City of Man. For example, look at the groundswell of antagonism against Jesus when it became apparent that he would not lead a movement founded on City-of-Man kind of strength. Or consider CNN's Ted Turner, who reportedly has called Christianity "a religion for losers." The City of Man sees the cross as the great consolation prize for those who just can't hack it in the City of Man.

THE CITY BUILT ON WEAKNESS

Actually, the realization that we can't hack it is a profound and true insight. All the striving and posturing and self-exalting that goes on in the City of Man is illusory. The issue is life: Who has it? Who can sustain it? Maslow said that the universal striving he observed in humanity was a striving for "autonomous life." Life is associated with virility, glory, wisdom, strength, and independence. It is a quality of God.

- We must acknowledge we do not have it.
- We must look to God for it.

These two principles are the bedrock foundation of the City of God. Those who wish to inherit this city are told by God to look to Abraham. He was an object lesson in this dynamic. Abraham literally could not produce life because Sarah, his wife, was barren. Yet God had promised that he would be the father of many nations.

What did Abraham do? Well, at first he tried to get the job done himself. He slept with his wife's maid and got her pregnant. But God explained that his promise wasn't going to be fulfilled that way. It was going to happen by the power of God.

Finally, Abraham gave it up. "He faced the fact that his body was as good as dead—since he was about a hundred years old—and that Sarah's womb was also dead" (Rom. 4:19). Recognizing his inability, he was forced to look at the promise of God—and to lean all his hope on God to accomplish what he, himself, could not do.

This dependence on God is the key to life. All of us are both invited and commanded to operate in everything as needy dependents—looking to God alone for help.

We mustn't conceive of his help as a boost up the ladder toward an independently secure and autonomous life. That's something we were never meant to have. Instead, he's calling us to a *dependent* life—a life that is being received from him continually. We don't have a hierarchy of needs; we have just one—God. In him we get everything we'll ever need.

LEARNING TO BE WEAK

Our sense of isolation doesn't give way easily. How can we become convinced at the deepest level that we are not orphans who must fend for ourselves? How can we believe that God is willing to help us? Our isolation from God runs even deeper than our isolation from humanity. Is he for me, or is he against me? Christian teaching says that God loves us, but our fears, insecurities, and feelings of aloneness seem to resist these reassurances.

Gina Cobb, Doug's wife, is a technical writer and is actively involved on the board of a mission agency. In spite of her competence and professionalism, however, she has struggled all her life to believe that God is accessible and willing to help her.

"I think I grew up with the idea that I was saved and would go to heaven, but until then I was pretty much on my own. God just wanted me to be good. Just keep the rules and don't get into trouble. There was never any sense that I could go to him for help," she says, "especially if I created the problems myself by procrastinating or something. They were my responsibility."[7]

Gina's struggle is rooted in something that's written on the conscience of humankind. Sometimes we're in a defensive mode; sometimes we're justifying ourselves—but in both responses we reveal that an unspoken demand weighs on us. At some level we know that God is our Judge and we've been sent out of the Garden. His judgment is real, and our isolation from him is not an illusion either. The sense that we are on our own in the cold, cruel world is grounded in reality. We need to come to grips with this fact in order to lay hold of the work of God—not as some false assurance that deceives our consciences, but as that which actually cleanses our consciences of any vestige of God's disapproval and clears the way for us to believe and receive the love of God for us.

A look at Mount Sinai gets our real need out on the table. Mount Sinai was where God gave the Israelites his law through Moses. With an awesome display of the holiness of his being—darkness, gloom, and storm—and warnings about the danger of sinful people approaching him, God made his righteous expectations known. "Do this, and you will live," is the message of the Law. But the people "could not bear what was commanded" (Heb. 12:20). At Mount Sinai there is a terrifying distance between us and God, and we are profoundly aware that his disapproval rightly rests on us.

But you have not come to Mount Sinai, Hebrews 12:22 says. "You have come to . . . the city of the living God." The City of God is a city of refuge from God's judgment. The "sprinkled blood" of Jesus has cleansed us of sin and opened the way for us to go amazingly near to him without fear of rejection. Because of what Jesus did, the relationship we have with God is free from all condemnation, all guilt, every demanding threat and judgment. He is a Father who delights in our company and promises to help us. His face is not frowning in disapproval. He isn't rolling his eyes in disappointment. His face is shining with love as he looks at us—because of what Jesus did. In the City of God, weakness does not draw forth contempt; it is met with loving compassion and mercy.

GOD'S OUTPOURING ON WEAKNESS

There is an outpouring of good to us in the City of God that reaches to the most basic needs we experience in the City of Man. Again and again Jesus tells us to trust the Father's love. "Would you give your son a stone if he asked for bread?" Jesus asked (see Matt. 7:9).

Jesus is very realistic about the fact that we are still *in* the City of Man where "need" defines our lives. "Each day has enough trouble of its own," he says (Matt. 6:34). However, he promises that the Father will supply our needs along the way as we make our pilgrimage to the fully realized and visible City of God. We can expect practical help with our practical needs.

Bob Byers and his wife, Joyce, own and operate Byers' Choice—a manufacturer of collectable figurines. Their line of whimsical Christmas carolers originated in Joyce's creative imagination and first found expression at their kitchen table. Byers' Choice is now the largest company of its kind in the market.

"Anyone who doesn't think the Lord wants to be involved in their business is making a terrible mistake," Bob says.[8] "The idea for Byers' Choice came after two miserable failures. I failed as a corporate leader, and I failed as an entrepreneur. My wife and I got down on our knees and pleaded with God for a livelihood. The idea for manufacturing Joyce's figurines came quickly after we finally went to him in total desperation.

"And we have continued to need him in every way. One day I was facing a dreadful business problem. I was sick with worry. I wasn't just thinking of myself; we have almost two hundred employees who depend on our company for a livelihood. Many of them have been with us for years. They're like family. So I was facing a horrendous possibility of everything collapsing. I didn't know what to do, and I had terrible thoughts of doing a highly illegal and sinful thing. It seemed like the only possible way out. I was overcome with temptation, so I fell on my hands and knees and asked God to take this overwhelming burden and get rid of the thoughts I was having. When I got up, he had done it. The burden was gone and I felt peace. Within a week the problem was solved in a way I never could have imagined."

Bob isn't ashamed to tell anybody and everybody who will listen that he is a miserable failure who has a wonderful God. He and Joyce have produced an illustrated book about the history of their company. On the first page of the first chapter, entitled "What Byers' Choice Is All About," are these words:

He will call upon me, and I will answer him;
I will be with him in trouble,
I will deliver him and honor him. (Ps. 91:15)

Bob's story illustrates the central dynamic of the relationship we have with our heavenly Father: "Ask and you will receive" (John 16:24). *Asking* acknowledges need and confidence in the willingness of our Father to help us. *Receiving* illustrates the lavish love of God for his children.

We aren't meant to take his promise of provision as an excuse to be idle or as our ticket to the indulgences the City of Man desires. His promise means we can stop expending all our energy and effort running after our needs like isolated orphans with no Father to provide for us.

THE FREEDOM OF BEING WEAK

"Come, all you who are thirsty, / come to the waters; / and you who have no money, / come, buy and eat! / Come, buy wine and milk / without money and without cost. . . . Delight in the richest of fare" (Isa. 55:1–2).

With these words Isaiah issues an invitation to anyone with need to come and find an overflow of supplies that don't cost anything. The apostle John closes the Book of Revelation with a description of the City of God as a place of abundance—where the tree of life grows on both sides of the river of life and bears twelve kinds of fruit every month. He reiterates Isaiah's words: "'Come!' Whoever is thirsty, let him come" (Rev. 22:17).

This is not an abundance of City-of-Man stuff; it's an abundance of the Spirit of God—an overwhelming flood of God himself. Jesus specifically contrasts the you-drink-and-get-thirsty-again water with the living water that will well up in us like a spring and flow out of us to others. But we must *ask*. That's what Jesus told the Samaritan woman. He told her that if she knew who he was, she would have asked him and he would have given her living water to drink.

Jesus emphasized the same thing in Luke 11. First he told a story that illustrated our empty-handedness when it comes to the things of the Kingdom. A man had friends come to visit him at midnight. He had nothing in the way of sustenance to offer them, so he ran to his neighbor and asked for something to put on the table. The neighbor was reluctant. But Jesus assures us that God— our Father—is not reluctant. "Ask and it will be given to you," Jesus says (v. 9). "If you then, though you are evil, know how to give good gifts . . . how much more will your Father in heaven give the Holy Spirit to those who ask him!" (v. 13).

Freedom from anxiety comes from laying our needs before our

Father and trusting him to provide. But that's not the end of it. Freedom from anxiety sets our hearts and energies loose for a purpose—to pursue the things of the City of God.

When Jesus was on the boat with his disciples, he told them to beware of the yeast of the Pharisees. They thought he was referring to the fact that they'd forgotten to bring bread. Jesus was incredulous! He asked them if they had so soon forgotten when he fed the five thousand from five loaves. He marveled that they could still be worried about bread. The fact is—we can be unafraid, self-revealing, and joyous because of the provision of God for us. As a result, our freedom from self-concern frees us to serve others.

This realization transformed Gina Cobb's life. "I have a whole new paradigm now—the gospel paradigm," she says. She no longer thinks of God as remote and shrouded in disapproval. "He loves me and he is interested in every little thing about me. My weakness doesn't separate him from me. It draws him to me in compassion. And when I share the gospel with other people, I'm not saying, 'Be like me.' I'm saying, 'I am weak just like you. Let me tell you where I found help.'"

Cecilia Chacon's life has also been profoundly affected in a similar way. Fast forward *two* years from moving day, and we'll see her standing on the corner of their property—in the same posh neighborhood—with a pitcher of lemonade, waiting to serve the garbage men on their twice-weekly route. She and her four-year-old came up with this ministry idea. Cecilia has also befriended a lonely, divorced neighbor. "People are just people," she says. "They all have needs."

What brought about this remarkable change? "I have the righteousness of Jesus," Cecilia explains as she breaks into a broad grin. "I am free! Why do I have to worry about what other people think when God does not judge me? For the first time, I have a Father who is always there when I need him. So I can stop thinking about myself all the time and just be a mother hen to other people!"

Chapter 5
Being Righteous

"On the outside you appear to people as righteous but on the inside you are full of . . . wickedness."
JESUS TO THE PHARISEES, MATTHEW 23:28

If you've seen the musical hit *Les Misérables*, you know that two characters are contrasted throughout the play—the hero, Jean Valjean, and his antagonist, Javert. As an instrument of the law, the policeman, Javert, is determined to bring the parole-breaker, Jean Valjean, to justice. For most of the musical, Javert never falters in his pursuit or his sense of integrity.

At one point the policeman sings a solo where he expresses the passion of his life: "Mine is the way of the Lord," he sings, "and those who follow the path of the righteous shall have their reward. And if they fall, as Lucifer fell—The flame! The sword."

Later in the play, however, Javert finds himself at Jean Valjean's mercy, and instead of killing him, the criminal spares the policeman's life and sets him free. Javert is utterly devastated. "Vengeance was his and he gave me my life!" he cries. "Shall his sins be forgiven? Shall his crimes be reprieved?"

His lifelong pursuit of rightness had brought him to a place he never in his worst nightmares expected to be—bested by the

63

very one he was convinced was his moral inferior. If Valjean, the criminal, is the better man, then the policeman's entire reason for existence, his very identity, is taken away. In fact, Javert ends up committing suicide.

Javert ran up against the catch-22 of pursuing a moral life. Although we intend to separate ourselves from evil and do what's right, we end up being in the wrong despite our determined efforts.

John Weiser didn't start off very concerned about doing what was right. He describes his college self as a "harmless, semi-wild, beer-drinking Indiana University student who just sat in the middle of the class and drifted through without flunking out."[1] After college he married his high school sweetheart and—because he didn't have any particular idea of what to do next—took his brother's advice and applied for a job in banking. He was hired at a bank in Cleveland, became a father, and did what decent, middle-of-the-road people did back then—he took his family to church. After a while he was asked to be a deacon. "I told them there was a little problem, because I didn't believe in God," John remembers. "But they said, 'That's all right, we just need some nice young people.' Before I knew it I was a deacon."

The next step was a move to Charlottesville, where success took John by surprise. He realized from his banking experience that he had a knack for investment, so he started his own investment company. In a very short time he was making a million a year. "I wasn't trying to be rich," John says. "I didn't crave it or think I deserved it. But when I suddenly found myself very wealthy, I thought, *Well, I won. I don't know how I did it, but this is the prize. I'm a winner.*"

But, as many wealthy people everywhere will attest, money doesn't buy happiness. John explains: "It just wasn't that big a deal. I really wasn't that happy.

"When I started wondering about religion, we were part of a church discussion group where no one was a Christian, not even the pastor," John recalls. "Even I realized they didn't have answers. So I decided to read the Bible, starting with page one. I read all the way to the end. I didn't have any agenda. I just asked God to show me if he was there. I wasn't going to get excited and try to convince myself."

Faith came to John sort of like success had—it just crept up on him from behind. He read a book by Christian philosopher Francis Schaeffer, and "suddenly I knew both the questions and the answers. It made perfect sense. My mind was brought to life. I had never read for fun—I just played sports and watched TV—but now I wanted to know everything there was to know about this Truth."

For the first time in his life John was really excited about something. He and his wife Terri attended classes at the Christian Study Center next to the University of Virginia—four days a week for four hours a day. In the meantime, the business lost a million dollars in a single day and eventually went broke. Since then he has made two moves and is now in Fort Worth, where he handles investment capital for the Bass Brothers and is again very successful. When they got to Fort Worth, he and Terri helped organize and finance a new church in the area. His greatest interest and the focus of his energies was the church.

A couple of years ago, however, John came to a devastating realization. He called up a Christian counselor and these were the first words out of his mouth: "I am a very successful man. But I don't love God, and I don't love anyone else either."

John could have attributed his coldheartedness to Christian maturity. The very fact that he was aware of it and grieved by it was a remarkable change from the unexamined conviction that he had everything down pat. He could have glossed over the commandments to love God with all our heart, soul, mind and strength and to love our neighbor as ourselves in the blindness that comes from doing and believing so much that is right. But he didn't. He realized that when he tried to love God, all he felt was a cold, flat nothingness. Loving his brothers and sisters in Christ? Well, he had to admit most of the time he was impatient with them for not measuring up, or else he was just downright bored by their company.

WHAT'S WRONG WITH THIS PICTURE?

"Why is it," an unbelieving son of a pastor once asked, "that people without absolute truth are often much kinder than people who think they know the truth?" Likewise, how was it that becoming a Christian had made John into a less gentle and sympathetic person than the laid-back unbelieving college student he had once been?

One answer is that the sort of kindness the City of Man wants is one that leaves people alone, that doesn't challenge or convict them. There is a reverse self-righteousness at work in the politically correct agenda—one that claims tolerance as the ultimate kindness. The pastor's son—the one who posed the question of why those without absolute truth are kinder—is infected with a sense of his own moral superiority. He is convinced that by not assuming the "judgmental" attitude he associates with his Christian upbringing he is the one in the right.

The trouble is the zeal to be right. The City of Man is driven by it. Immorality is justified. Selfish actions are defended. Excuses are made. Blame is shifted. Fingers point. We love the glory of being right. The temptation to which our first parents succumbed was the opportunity to be like God—not in his power and eternity but as an authority on moral excellence, knowing good and evil. This tendency is especially evident in religion. Buddhists, Hindus, Jews, Muslims, and many Christians are pursuing rightness with a drive that only moral absolutes can fuel.

What happens is this: we see what is actually true and good—that which God himself has revealed, either through the conscience of man or directly in his law—and we go for it. But we go for it with the self-exalting attitude of the City of Man that is innate to all of us. The goal is measured like everything in the City of Man—by comparison to others. We become religiously competitive. The sense of approval we crave is the sense of being at the top. Righteousness is just one more way we climb the ladder. The prize? Being in a position to judge. The further we progress up that ladder, the further we get from true righteousness.

Nonetheless, backing off from moral absolutes is not the answer. The answer lies somewhere else.

CLIMBING THE RELIGIOUS LADDER

Jesus was having a discussion one day with an expert in the law of God. This man wanted to test Jesus' knowledge, so he asked him, "What must I do to inherit eternal life?" In response, Jesus asked a question of his own, "What is written in the Law? . . . How do you read it?" The man gave the right answer: "'Love the Lord your God with all your heart and with all your soul and with all your strength and with all your mind'; and, 'Love your neighbor as yourself.'" Jesus agreed with him that these are the moral absolutes: "Do this and you will live." But then the man, wanting "to justify himself," asked, "Who is my neighbor?" (Luke 10:25–37).

This teacher of the Law was looking at things with his City-of-Man glasses. He wanted to gain life, and he realized it required being righteous. Therefore, his entire life and all his energies were devoted to justifying himself, to climbing the religious ladder. He probably reasoned with himself as follows:

"Loving God? OK, I think I've got that one down. After all, I am very religious. The motive of my life is to be approved by God. Now, what about this matter of loving my neighbor? Let me make sure I understand that because I don't want to be found at fault here. There could be something I've missed, although I doubt it. Who exactly is this neighbor I'm supposed to love?"

The man didn't have the first clue about loving other people because his motive was fundamentally self-centered. He was self-absorbed, self-approving, and self-serving. Whatever sacrifices he might make in the name of love would always curve right back onto himself.

We are all caught in the same dilemma. We cannot bear to see this truth because we are driven to justify ourselves. Whether we are able to articulate it or not, at some level we know that to be found at fault by God will be eternally deadly. When the standards of righteousness are presented to us, we feel judgment threatening and we go into a self-defense mode: "Please define this requirement in concrete terms so I can get it down. Who exactly am I supposed to love, and what specifically am I supposed to do?"

In answer to the man's question, Jesus tells a story: A man is beaten, robbed, and left for dead. Two very religious people pass by him without stopping to help. The third man, a Samaritan (someone this teacher of the Law would consider so far beneath him that he would not even taint himself by touching the guy) stops and helps the man. The Samaritan's love is unstinting, practical, and deeply compassionate.

Jesus seems to be saying two things with this story: First—he is demonstrating that the requirement to love is far greater than this man's law-limiting, self-justifying attitude could ever have imagined. And second—he seems to be making the point that *people who seek to justify themselves will never be able to love.*

The apostle Paul felt the hopelessness of untying this Gordian knot. "The commandment is holy, righteous and good," he says (Rom. 7:12). But the commandment "Thou shalt not covet" is one he could never keep. It cuts to the core of our being and exposes us. "Wanting" is our middle name. There is nothing in us that is untainted by our inherent self-serving bent.

We may control our outward actions, but our hearts are polluted and we can find no motive that is selfless. And when we see this about ourselves, we die. We are condemned. "Who will rescue me?" Paul pleads (Rom. 7:24). What cuts the Gordian knot?

NO MORE CONDEMNATION

The answer, he says, is this: "There is now no condemnation" (Rom. 8:1).

To know that there is no hope of self-justification, to know that one deserves death, and yet to receive mercy instead, to have the condemnation removed and blessing poured out in its place—this is the thing that writes love upon the heart.

Jesus encountered many individuals who were blinded by their sense of self-justification. One was a man named Simon. Simon was a Pharisee as well as a wealthy man. His self-approval was buffered by the approval of his neighbors, not only because he was very religious, but also because he was a man of means.

One day Simon decided to hold a dinner party. He invited Jesus to come, probably to check him out. Jesus had been creating quite a stir in the region. He was being followed around by multitudes of people—most of them uneducated, some of them reputed to be the worst kind of sinners. As a religious leader, Simon was obligated to come to some conclusion about Jesus. If he was a prophet, Simon needed to find out, maybe even lend him his support. If Jesus was just a charlatan, then the sooner Simon denounced him, the better.

The biblical account in Luke 7 gives the impression that Simon thought he was doing Jesus a favor. Although he invited Jesus to dinner, he didn't extend to him the required courtesies that any guest could expect. In that culture, a guest was honored by a basin of water to wash his dusty feet, a touch of oil on the head, and a kiss of greeting. Simon didn't offer any of these things to Jesus.

The table where dinner was served was low to the ground, and people reclined on the floor when they ate. A woman who had a terrible reputation in the town, no doubt for sexual sin, had heard where Jesus was having dinner and had come there to see him. She was probably a prostitute. At any rate, she broke in on the dinner party and proceeded to remedy Simon's rude omissions. She cleaned Jesus' dusty feet with her own tears, wiped them with her hair, kissed them, and poured perfume on them.

Simon knew a sinner when he saw one, and he made up his mind instantly about Jesus: "If this man were a prophet, he would know who is touching him and what kind of a woman she is" (v. 39).

Jesus then proceeded to illustrate how Simon, a man who had devoted his whole life to being on God's side, had ended up being outdone by a gross sinner.

"Simon," Jesus said, "I have something to tell you."

"Tell me," Simon said.

"Two men owed money to a certain moneylender. One owed him five hundred denarii [a denarius was a coin worth about one day's wages], and the other fifty. Neither of them had the money to pay him back, so he canceled the debts of both. Now which of them will love him more?" (v. 41).

Simon answered with some reluctance. Maybe he realized he was being set up. "I suppose the one who had the bigger debt canceled," he said (v. 43).

"You have judged correctly," Jesus tells him. And then he turned to the sinful woman and he said, "Do you see this woman? I came into your house. You did not give me any water for my feet, but she wet my feet with her tears" (v. 43–44). Jesus went on to contrast the woman's excessive outpouring of love for him to Simon's stingy rudeness.

In that story, Jesus gave Simon the key: *The one who loves God is the one who realizes that he has been forgiven much.* Jesus equated loving God with loving himself. Jesus was the Son of God. He was standing in Simon's presence, and Simon not only didn't love Jesus; he didn't even have the decency to show him common courtesy. How could Simon have blown it so completely?

God comes as a mercy-giver. Jesus is God's communication to the City of Man, and he will not be beautiful to us unless we know we need what he has come to give. If we are blinded by a sense of being right, we will not love God. Loving God comes when we realize our unpayable debt (finally admitting that being right is out of the question) and see that Jesus has taken care of it for us—he has paid our debt.

Look at the sinful woman. We need to be very clear about one thing first of all. She *was* a sinner. Jesus didn't dismiss her sin as unimportant. In fact, he said that her sin had created a great debt. Moral absolutes have divine authority. But she also knew that Jesus, unlike all the other religious people she had ever known, was a friend of sinners. She was immune to the opinion of everyone else in the room, including the judgment of Simon the Pharisee. She only had eyes for Jesus. Jesus looked directly at her and, in a conversation that excluded everyone else in the room, a conversation that was just between the Lord and the sinner, he told her, "Your sins are forgiven" (v. 48). There is no more condemnation.

This woman, unlike Simon, realized that she had no rights to God, no reason to expect anything but rejection, and so she was overwhelmed that Jesus received her. Maybe she even had some clue that the feet she washed would be pierced to pay her debt. In any case, she loved Jesus much. They had a relationship of mutual delight—she loving him, not caring who knew about it, and he delighting in her love, forgiving all her sins, owning her as his friend before the condemning eyes of Simon the Pharisee. Mercy created love for Jesus in her heart.

This was Jean Valjean's secret as well. *Les Misérables*, the musical, captures the essential theme Victor Hugo develops in his novel. Jean Valjean had been condemned by the law as a thief. He was angry, bitter, defensive—self-justifying. When he was finally released on parole, every door slammed in his face. As an ex-con, he was shunned and rejected by the upstanding citizens of the city—everyone, that is, except a bishop of the church who received him into his home, shared his table with him, and then offered him a bed for the night.

Jean was deeply moved that the bishop called him *Monsieur*—a term of honor and respect—yet he resisted this kindness. His heart was too hard. His anger at injustice too deep. Instead of being grateful, Valjean stole away during the night with the bishop's silver cutlery. When the police dragged him back with the evidence, the bishop surprised them by explaining that the silver had actually been intended as a gift and then added grace upon grace by giving Jean Valjean his silver candlesticks.

After the policemen left, the bishop quietly said to Valjean, "Jean Valjean, my brother: you belong no longer to evil, but to good. It is your soul I am buying for you. I withdraw it from dark thoughts and from the spirit of perdition, and I give it to God!"[2] Essentially, the bishop's actions were a picture of the cross.

What did Jean Valjean do? He ran away. He was stunned. He had been robbed of his self-justification. He knew he had received a reprieve from a punishment that he fully deserved. He felt that "the priest's pardon was the hardest assault, the most formidable attack he had ever sustained; that his hardness of heart would be complete if it resisted this kindness. And that if he yielded, he would have to renounce hatred. . . . It was either conquer or be conquered."[3]

In a final transforming capitulation, Jean Valjean allowed himself to be broken by mercy and captured by the love of God. Being right . . . self-justification . . . they were gone forever. What the law could not do, mercy accomplished.

LIVING IN NEED OF MERCY

In Les Misérables, Jean Valjean never moved away from this identity. He was never a righteous man in his own sight. He was forever one who had received mercy. So when his enemy, Javert, was caught in his clutches and he had every excuse to take his life, Jean Valjean extended mercy instead. A man who lives in need of mercy does not withhold it from others.

JOHN'S STORY ... CONTINUED

Unfortunately, most Christians, even if we start off transformed by mercy, shift. A wise Christian counselor helped John Wieser realize he had shifted. "The problem was that I left the cross back at conversion. After that I started pursuing excellence. I wanted to be an excellent Christian."

Somewhere along the way John lost the sense that he had been forgiven much. He regained it by seeing his "Pharisee" sins, seeing that self-righteousness had made his heart grow cold toward the mercy of Jesus. He had become a blind guide, leading other people into a life of "being right," rather than to Jesus, the friend of sinners. He was quick to assess, to argue, and to condemn. In his pursuit of excellence he had gained a great deal of knowledge and had chalked up a lot of good deeds—and had become a "small debt" sinner. And in seeing this—with a swift stroke that cut the Gordian knot in his Christian life—John also saw the mercy of God for him afresh. Jesus paid the debt for his "Pharisee" sins on the cross! When he saw the price of his forgiveness, love for God flowed back into his life.

SUSAN'S STORY

Susan Nikaido, senior editor of *Discipleship Journal*, a publication of the Navigators, tells a story similar to John's:

> I'd rather not think about my sin. In fact, I'd
> rather pretend it isn't there. It's much easier to
> call my lack of obedience a "failure," "mistake,"
> or "slip," brushing it quickly away with a resolve
> to do better next time. When I first heard the
> gospel explained clearly at age 16, it was the
> hardest thing for me to grasp that I was a sinner
> in need of a Savior. After all, I was a good girl. I
> was blessed with a strict conscience, which I
> rarely violated. I didn't even let my friends use

my 4-H pass to get into the fairgrounds, let alone venture into the deeper waters of teenage trespasses. At that point, accepting my sinfulness took almost as much faith as accepting Jesus' salvation.

I suspect that, though we know the verses that say otherwise, a lot of us still like to think of ourselves as "good people." We are driven by the desire to do the right thing, and we have been mostly successful. We're nice to people, we are diligent employees, and we do our share at church and in the community. We stay away from what society considers the big sins. So if we gossip a little, or are critical of others, or ignore that prompting to mow the elderly neighbor's lawn, it's really not that big a deal . . . is it? Taking time to reflect on our pride, our selfishness, and our lack of faith would threaten that image we like to hold of ourselves. But, if I'm reluctant to look at my sinfulness, I'll never deeply grasp or experience the wonderful grace of God.

Since my dry-eyed conversion, I've always kind of envied those people who weep at the altar rail and rise with shining faces. I've wondered why I wasn't able to muster as much emotion as they did. Throughout my Christian life, I have occasionally been troubled that many others seem to experience a love for Jesus much deeper than mine. . . . I am seeing now that holding on to my "good person" self-image has squeezed a lot of life out of my relationship with God. If we dare ask God to help us see our sinfulness, I can attest that He will be faithful to show us! It is a risk well worth taking. Rather than a discipline to be avoided, confession can become the time when our hearts are moved most deeply by the wonder of His mercy, forgiveness, and love.[4]

CHUCK'S STORY

Around the turn of the century, a counterfeiter was operating in a remote area of Louisiana making twenty-dollar bills. He did it by painting each one on both sides. It boggles the imagination to think of the time and talent it must have taken for him to make these almost perfect duplications of the real thing. However, when the authorities finally caught up with him, they weren't impressed with his artistic ability. His bills were fake, and he was guilty.

Chuck DeBardeleben also was a kind of counterfeiter. When he graduated from seminary, he had two goals. "They were not conscious goals, but they ruled my life. The first one was to 'be right' and the second one was to 'look good.'"[5] He worked, as he puts it, "impossible hours." When his wife complained, he told her, "I'm doing the Lord's work." His church in the Florida panhandle doubled in size in ten years, and he developed a reputation for being a good pastor. Unfortunately his accomplishments were like those phony twenty-dollar bills—convincing fakes that even managed to fool Chuck himself.

The rightness we produce is inevitably a counterfeit. It becomes a deceiving cover for the rotten motivations underneath. When Chuck began to see just a little bit of the bankruptcy of his heart, he felt as if his world was crumbling. He would not have been able to endure the exposure if it hadn't happened while he was simultaneously seeing and understanding the grace of God for him.

"One day I was driving over the Pensacola Bridge, and I was overtaken by the love of God. At the same time I was seeing my sins exposed in the full light of day, but it didn't hurt so much because his love was so great."

Chuck started relating to people differently as a result.

"There was a deaf woman in my church. When I first came as pastor, she explained that she was deaf and asked me if I would give her an outline of the sermon each week since she couldn't pick up everything from reading lips. When I mentioned this to one of my elders, he said, 'This is great. This woman and her husband are big givers, and they were about to leave the church.'

"I thought to myself, *Bingo!* I not only gave her an outline, I spent hours typing up a full transcript of the sermon. Along with many other sins, the Lord finally showed me how hypocritical and self-centered I had been with this woman. I asked her to come and see me, and when she came to my office, I wrote her a little note explaining how I had manipulated her out of fear and pride. We both cried. It was a wonderful meeting."

Chuck was the genuine article with this woman. He wasn't driven to hide his sins anymore. He wasn't carefully trying to paint a really good imitation of righteousness. He was free to let her see the evil in his heart because the agenda had changed. He wanted Jesus to get all the glory.

Jesus said that people hide from the light because they are evil and they don't want to be exposed. But those who live by the truth come to the light—they freely expose their sins "so that it may be seen plainly that what he has done has been done through God" (John 3:21).

The apostle Paul declared that he was the foremost of sinners for whom Christ died (1 Tim. 1:15–17). This was the identity, the operating dynamic, that produced a life poured out for God and other people. It was the reality that enabled Paul to say, "You know we never used flattery, nor did we put on a mask to cover up greed—God is our witness" (1 Thess. 2:5).

To the end of his life, Paul was throwing away his bragging rights, calling all his right-ness nothing but garbage. His goal had changed from "looking good" and "being right." He was compelled by the love of Christ to direct attention away from himself to the one who died for sinners.

THE ETHICS OF THE CITY OF GOD

God chiseled the Ten Commandments on tablets of stone, but, Paul says, he has written the gospel as a letter on our hearts (2 Cor. 3:2ff). James calls it "the law that gives freedom" (James 2:12). The very message that embraces us with Christ's sacrifice of love—that teaches us that we have no righteousness but, to the contrary, that we are so unrighteous that this sacrifice was required in order for us to be forgiven; and that gives us freedom from the drive to justify ourselves—also produces love for God and for other people in our hearts. What could only be commanded is now fulfilled in us.

"Love your neighbor as yourself" runs counter to everything that drives the City of Man. Only a cataclysmic event could alter us—break us out of the natural bent to love only ourselves. Compassion and mercy—undeserved, costing the Son of God unimaginable suffering, offered freely, offered in infinite love—this is how God has rocked the earth. He has shaken it to the foundations. He has radically altered us with this love. In fact, he has actually "killed" us and brought us to life again. He has transferred us out of the City of Man into the City of God where "mercy triumphs over judgment!" (James 2:13)

In the City of Man, our self-justifying agenda puts a barrier between us and other people—"the dividing wall of hostility" Paul calls it (Eph. 2:14). We are in competition with each other. We judge each other. We feel superior to each other. We are insincere with each other. But this whole agenda has been removed by Christ's death. The issue of justification has been settled in our favor, not on the basis of our rightness, but on the basis of Christ's righteousness. In the process, we have died and been regenerated as people who are free to identify with others and reveal ourselves to them as fellow sinners—and to love them.

Jesus tells us that if we love him we will love each other. When we don't love, it is because our faith is weak. We have forgotten the identity that belongs to each of us—the chief of sinners saved by the cross. Our love for Jesus has grown cold.

Jesus says that if we come to the end of our days and have not shown mercy to others, having collected debts instead of forgiving them, then he will say he never knew us. If we have been indifferent, coldhearted people-haters, this will prove that we have not believed at a deep level, and like Simon the Pharisee, we have not known Jesus.

Since Pharisaism is the condition we naturally slide toward—like addicts who take a hit of self-righteousness before we know what we're doing—repentance and faith must be our daily operating procedure. We daily acknowledge sin and embrace the cross. We daily are restored to the reality that we are big-debt sinners who have been loved much! And this faith expresses itself in love for other people. If we love Jesus, we have no option but to get on board what he is doing. He himself has left us no option but to join him in loving people. But it is the Spirit who produces this love—Christ's love—in us as he plants the gospel more deeply in our hearts.

John Weiser says, "I realize now that the Christian life is a life of repentance and faith. The other day I was just walking down the sidewalk, and I started hating the guy in front of me. I didn't know him. I couldn't even see his face, but I just didn't like the way he carried himself. I am so much more aware now of how evil my heart is. I don't kid myself that I am naturally a nice guy. I need Jesus all the time. So I repented on the spot. I just said,

'Lord, forgive me; I hate this guy.' And the Lord changed my heart—right there. I looked at the guy's back, and I had compassion for him."

John has a new ministry in the church he helped to found— he brings the gospel to believers, leading them to see afresh that Jesus is a friend to sinners and that self-righteousness is the most blinding and ugly sin around because it denies the value and necessity of the cross.

Chapter 6
Going Under

"A new command I give you: Love one another."
JESUS TO HIS DISCIPLES, JOHN 13:34

Success. The word comes from two Latin words meaning "going beneath."

The idea of going beneath couldn't be further from what the City of Man thinks of as success. We think of it more like "going above." Associating success with "going lower," much less "going under," is a completely foreign concept. All our efforts and energies are devoted to scrambling up.

However, Jesus gave *success* in the City of God a radically different definition—one that is closer to the word's original Latin roots: "For he who is least among you all—he is the greatest" (Luke 9:48); "The last will be first, and the first will be last" (Matt. 20:16); "The man who loves his life will lose it, while the man who hates his life in this world will keep it" (John 12:25); "The greatest among you will be your servant" (Matt. 23:11).

Jesus wasn't just coming up with clever paradoxes. He was explaining the measurement of success he would establish by his own actions. The definition of success in the City of God is simply: What Jesus did. The actions Jesus took didn't merely adjust and refine the City of Man's idea of success. They reversed it. In fact, they overthrew it. If we want to live in the City of Man as citizens of the City of God, we must understand that the ideas of success in these two cities are diametrically opposed to each other. One has been exposed and judged by the cross while the other has been eternally established and approved of by the cross. We must choose which city's success we will pursue.

Just before Jesus was crucified he gave a deliberate demonstration of City-of-God success. The scene was the upper room. He and the disciples had gathered to eat the Passover meal on the night of his arrest. Before the meal, Jesus removed his robe, took a towel, and wrapped it around his waist—dressing himself like a typical servant of the day. Then he took a basin of water and knelt before each disciple, washing their feet and drying them with the towel. This most menial act was performed even for Judas, whom Jesus knew was about to betray him. Kneeling to wash someone's feet is a picture that needs little explanation. It's seen as a menial task in any culture, the act of a servant who exists for the sake of others.

After Jesus finished washing the disciples' feet, he put his clothes back on and returned to his place at the table. He then explained why he had done this outrageous thing.

JESUS EXPLAINS CITY-OF-GOD SUCCESS

"You call me 'Teacher' and 'Lord,' and rightly so," Jesus said (John 13:13).

He confirmed that there are legitimate hierarchies. Teachers are above their students. Bosses are above their employees. Parents are above their children. Kings are above their subjects. These aren't hierarchies of actual value. The teacher doesn't have more worth in God's eyes. God does not make those kinds of distinctions between people. He doesn't consider one person of more significance or importance than another. But he has established roles that are invested by him with authority, thereby commanding honor and obedience. God calls us to give "honor to whom honor is due" (Rom. 13:7 RSV).

All authority ultimately resides in Jesus as King of kings, and every other authority is derived from him. All honor, glory, power, and praise are his by right. He is the heavyweight.

Jesus says, "I, your Lord and teacher, have washed your feet" (John 13:14). In other words, "I have taken off my robe and with it all the rights and privileges of my position, and I have made myself your servant."

John tells us that Jesus did this for two reasons: First, he wanted us to understand that he loves his own to the uttermost. Second, he wanted to give us an example. "I have set you an example that you should do as I have done for you" (John 13:15). "You also should wash one another's feet" (John 13:14).

Then he adds the kicker: "No servant is greater than his master, nor is a messenger greater than the one who sent him" (John 13:16). If we want to go lower than Jesus was willing to go, we will find it impossible. But if we refuse—if we hang on to our own glory—we will be presuming to place ourselves higher than Jesus placed himself.

Jesus explained this idea of servanthood on another occasion, when James and John had come to him with a request. They knew he would one day establish his Kingdom, and that, like all kings, he would appoint his loyal followers to positions of high rank. James and John wanted to be on top.

"Teacher," they said, "we want you to do for us whatever we ask" (Mark 10:35).

"What do you want me to do for you?" Jesus asked (v. 36).

"Let one of us sit at your right and the other at your left in your glory" (v. 37). Like good citizens of the City of Man, they were ambitious for themselves. They wanted the glory that comes from being elevated above everyone else. Not above Jesus, of course. He would be number one. Number two and number three would be fine.

Jesus patiently explained to them the difference between the City of God and the City of Man. In the City of Man the leaders and rulers lord it over others, and they make use of their positions to exalt themselves and to be served by others. In the City of God, however, the one who wants to be great must be a servant, and the one who wants to be first must be a slave to all.

"Even the Son of Man," Jesus said, "did not come to be served, but to serve, and to give his life as a ransom for many" (Mark 10:45). Jesus' servanthood was radical. He came down from the highest place in the City of God to the place of ultimate degradation in the City of Man for the express purpose of lifting us up and sharing his exaltation with us. In so doing, he has pronounced judgment once and for all on the City of Man's concept of success.

We usually think of Jesus' servant role as drawing to a conclusion after the cross, but in reality, Jesus is still serving us as Priest and Intercessor, and he will serve us for eternity. Jesus said that when we all sit down at the feast of the visible, consummated City of God, he will wrap a towel around himself and wait on us. Glory and serving are eternally united in the City of God. This is the picture of greatness that Jesus presents to us: the slain lamb upon the throne—humility enthroned. It will call forth our exultant praise forever.

Jesus, by his actions, has established an everlasting precept: *Humble serving for the sake of exalting others is true glory.* The reverse, of course, is also true: *Self-serving for the sake of self-exaltation is true shame.*

LOVING OUR FRIENDS

Howard Butt is vice chairman of the board of his family's Texas business. H. E. Butt Grocery Company was started by his dad, "the classic inner-directed American entrepreneur, founder, chief stock-holder, and H.E.B. food stores' last word."[1]

Howard began his career in the family business when he was nine—stocking shelves and sweeping floors. By the time he was twelve he had gained the rank of cashier after memorizing the price of every item in the store. But as a young adult, his time and energies were divided between his position in the company and his leadership in two lay Christian ministries—Laity Lodge Foundation and Christian Men, Incorporated.

Unlike Howard, his younger brother, Charles, was going all-out for the company, working long hours with single-minded zeal and inherent ability. Even Howard agreed that his brother was the obvious choice to succeed their dad. Success in ministry became a subtle but critical salve for Howard's wounded pride. He carved a niche in Christian service where he could compete on his own ground. Eventually he planned to write a book and firmly establish himself as "somebody" in the arena of Christian ministry.

But before Howard got around to writing, a coworker announced that *he* was writing a book. The possibility that Keith might achieve the status of "published author" ahead of Howard felt like a blow to the gut. This was a brother-friend, someone he loved, someone he probably would have been willing to die for. Yet resentment gnawed away at him.

Finally, another friend confronted Howard about his obvious jealousy: "Why don't you accept your place? Your greatness is to make Keith great."

Jesus said there is no greater love than to lay down your life for your friend. When we hear this, we usually think of scenarios of glorious martyrdom, like throwing ourselves in front of a bullet. Welcoming obscurity for the sake of another isn't what we envision however. That's a death that goes deeper than bodily annihilation—asking us to give up the very identity we inherently strive to achieve and maintain. To do it successfully we must find a new identity—one where we are identified with Jesus in his death. For Howard it meant going down—going under—and lifting up his friend. It meant loving Keith as he loved himself, delighting in Keith's greatness as he would his own.

The City of Man impels us to fight tooth and nail for our own life and glory. The "boastful pride of life" (1 John 2:16 NASB) is what drives the world. It is what pits us one against another. Yet in the City of God we are called to give up the very thing we are fully energized to obtain and maintain. We must do so in order to love. Love requires a profound humbling that we just can't accomplish by ourselves. The trouble, Martin Luther said, is that we try to change while keeping ourselves intact. Hypocrisy is the inevitable result. We can create an appearance of love, but we can't love because we can't die.

When Howard realized what "dying for his friend" really meant, he was stuck. The thing was impossible. He couldn't do it. Yet he knew he had to do it.

Caught between his own inability and the unequivocal command of Jesus to lay down his life for his friend, Howard was driven to pray: "Lord Jesus, I commit to you my feelings about Keith and his book. I'm helpless to handle this on my own.

Thank you for handling it in your death and resurrection. Amen."[2]

Jesus did handle it. Within a few days Howard was able to confess his jealousy to Keith, and they had a good laugh. The power to love comes to us from Jesus. Both his death and his life are at work in us.

The surprising thing we discover on the other side of death is joy. "The best part for me," Howard said about Keith's best-selling book, "was my elation about Keith's success."

Howard made a profound shift from City-of-Man thinking—"It's all about me"—to City-of-God thinking—"It's all about you." He entered into the death of Christ in order to lift up his friend, and he found two things: a joyous fellowship with Jesus and a genuine love for his friend that enabled him to exult in Keith's victory.

Paul told the Philippians, "Your attitude should be the same as that of Christ Jesus: Who, being in very nature God, / did not consider equality with God something to be grasped, / but made himself nothing, / taking the very nature of a servant" (Phil. 2:5–7).

The reason we can humble ourselves without being infuriated by the humiliation is that we have been exalted by Christ. We have been enthroned with him, and our "going under" is not a groveling attempt to please nor a fear-driven submission. It's a choice we make. We choose to identify ourselves with the suffering love of Jesus in order to come to the party of joy he is hosting.

LOVING OUR ENEMIES

Jesus not only tells us to lay down our lives for our friends, but he commands us to love our enemies and do good to those who harm us. Who exactly is this enemy I'm supposed to love? Unfortunately, he isn't just Adolph Hitler or Saddam Hussein. My enemy is a person in my life: the guy I'm pitted against; the one whose gain is my loss; the one I need to prove is wrong so I can be vindicated; the one who's messing up my world. It's actually a lot easier to love a Saddam Hussein who is halfway around the world and unknown to me than to love the enemy in my family and at my job.

Remember Jeff Comment from chapter 1?[3] His enemy was the Teamster Union's local president. As far as Jeff was concerned, he was one bad guy. He had seriously imperiled Jeff's bid for success and caused a lot of misery and anguish, not to mention having said some pretty nasty things about Jeff personally.

When the dust settled after the strike settlement, Jeff gave some serious thought to his previously unexamined pursuit of success. It occurred to him that he needed to rethink his goals. Plunging headlong on an ego-driven bid for the top hadn't worked out too well. After humble self-examination, Jeff gave *success* a new definition. From then on Jeff was determined to measure his success by a new criterion: doing what pleases God. He was tentatively feeling his way as a manager whose primary objective was success in God's eyes when a Christian friend asked him a pointed question: "Jeff, have you talked to the Teamsters' local president since the strike?"

At first Jeff dismissed the idea as preposterous. But as he considered the commands to love his enemy, to forgive, and to not harbor anger, the idea became less absurd. Finally, Jeff decided it was actually necessary—in light of his new definition of success. He realized he couldn't just rearrange the furniture of his heart. To love his enemy he had to move toward him. That would mean relinquishing his deeply felt right to hate this man and being willing instead to see him as a person, not a stereotypical villain. Jeff had to come down from his identity of being the one who was wronged and listen to the other man's side and try to understand.

"After several days of procrastination," Jeff recalls, "I called the teamster and asked him to lunch. I think he was as surprised to receive my call as I was to make it. Our lunch turned out to be a three-hour affair, with more great Italian dishes than I knew existed."

What Jeff discovered tempered his judgment of the president's actions. He didn't agree with all the principles at work in the Teamsters' decision to strike, but he was able to understand and sympathize with their point of view. Jeff calmly shared his own perspective, not to counter and disprove the other man's convictions, but so they could have a common understanding. The talk eventually turned to their families and (to Jeff's surprise) their mutual faith in God.

"At the end of the lunch, we shook hands," Jeff says, "and agreed never to take an action involving the other without first sitting down and talking face to face."

Jeff's enemy became his friend because he had honored him as a friend. He was willing to see him as a person apart from their conflict and to listen to him with respect.

What we're really learning to do when we're learning to love is learning to look—to see people. Usually we maneuver through a day focused on getting our stuff done. People are either irrelevant to our agenda, a means to an end, or an impediment. We value them according to their function in our lives. We do not see them as valuable in their own right.

When the old Puritan writers spoke of *disinterested love,* they meant a love that doesn't see people through the lens of one's own interests. Love is profoundly interested in the other person. When we love, we set aside our own concerns and focus on someone else. We take on the weight of their world. *They* are the issue.

LOVING THE ONES UNDER US

John D. Beckett is president of R. W. Beckett Corporation in Elyria, Ohio. His company is the largest manufacturer of residential oil burners in the world. A graduate of MIT, John employs more than five hundred people. When "ABC News" interviewed him in 1995, they wanted to produce a feature about how he related his faith to his management. The interviewer asked him point-blank, "How is your business different as a result of trying to apply biblical principles?"

"The difference," John explained, "is how we regard people. I think the key issue is to see people as God sees them. When I saw this, it really changed the way I viewed not only myself but other people. I concluded I must place a high value on each person and never look down on another, regardless of their station in life. There's something sacred about every individual. Since God attributes unique and infinite worth to the individual, each one deserves our profound respect."[4]

While the City of Man places relative value on individuals depending on their status in the system, God considers people as the most important thing in creation regardless of their status. Each one has great weight and significance.

We see as God sees when we look at each individual with respect. "Honor all," the apostle says in 1 Peter 2:17 (NASB). Give them weight and significance in your estimation. Don't look past them; look *at* them and see something that is infinitely precious. If they are a brother or sister in Christ, see them as worth their weight in gold—purchased by the blood of Jesus.

Love bestows an exalted identity.

Love also enters into the loved one's world. Just as Jesus came into our world to share our lot and bear our burdens, we, too, take on the concerns, pains, and joys of other people.

Often we will see pain, discouragement, loneliness, fatigue, fear, or even less appealing things like anger, self-righteousness, and greed. When Jesus looked at people, he saw them as sheep without a shepherd to care for them. They were harassed and helpless, and his heart went out to them. He looked at the crowds who followed him into the wilderness, and he had compassion on them. They were hungry and it was a two-day journey to the nearest town, so he fed them.

When Jesus entered the city of Nain and saw the widow in the funeral procession of her only son, his eyes fixed on her. His face softened with tenderness. He entered into her world and identified with her from the heart. Then he brought her son back from the dead and gave him to her.

Jesus' entire life was poured out in love. In trying to understand the purpose of our own lives, it becomes very simple when we realize we are called into communion with Jesus to live a life of love. "Let's you and me love this person," Jesus is saying to us. "I will share my point of view with you. When you see him through my eyes, he will be precious to you, and your heart will go out to him."

Ephesians 5:1 captures the idea in a single sentence: "Live a life of love, just as Christ loved us and gave himself up for us."

One day a Roman centurion came to Jesus to plead for his dying servant. Jesus simply said, "I will go and heal him" (Matt. 8:7). But the centurion stopped him.

"Lord, I do not deserve to have you come under my roof. But just say the word, and my servant will be healed. For I myself am a man under authority, with soldiers under me. I tell this one, 'Go,' and he goes; and that one, 'Come,' and he comes. I say to my servant, 'Do this,' and he does it" (Matt. 8:5–10).

Jesus was astonished. The centurion was a man who understood authority. He realized it meant real power to compel obedience. He knew that he himself was under authority and that he also had authority over other people. His servant, for instance, did what he told him to do.

But the centurion loved his servant. He came personally out into the crowds of people and humbled himself before Jesus to intercede on his servant's behalf because he recognized that Jesus had an even greater authority. The faith that so astounded Jesus in this man was his recognition that Jesus' ability to heal came from his authority to command the Creation. The centurion knew authority when he saw it. He recognized that Jesus was the Author of life who was exercising his powerful prerogative to bring mercy. He was the King using his authority to serve.

According to Augustine, authority exercised in the City of God differs from the City of Man because "even those who rule serve those whom they seem to command; for they rule not from a love of power, not because they are proud of authority, but because they love mercy."[5]

Modeling Jesus, John Beckett has put his authority to use for the sake of his employees in practical, merciful ways. Recognizing that in the first three years of a child's life it is critical for the baby to bond with his mother, the company has a policy of allowing an employee one quarter pay for twenty-six weeks and lending them another quarter. Then they can return to work part-time, with the option of doing work at home for up to three years. When Chuck and Patty Visocky wanted to adopt four orphans from Columbia, they were given paid time off for the adoption trip. The company provides any parent one thousand dollars for each adopted child. When Eric Hess decided his promotion to lab technician just wasn't right for him, he was allowed to return to his former position. In time, Eric concluded that he was suited for a supervisory role. The company tested him for aptitude in this area and, when he showed promise, put him in a fully paid educational program for supervisors.

Loving leadership says, "My glory is to see you shine."

Whether we are parents, bosses, teachers, or church leaders, we don't relinquish our authority in order to serve those under us. We employ it for their good—to go under and raise them up.

When the Corinthians were dishonoring Paul's apostolic role, Paul defended it. He knew he had a God-given responsibility for them that was essential to their well-being and that he couldn't exercise that trust unless they respected his position. His motive wasn't to lord it over them. His goal was to fully confide in them the confidences he had received from Jesus—to see them become "kings so that we might be kings with you!" (1 Cor. 4:8). He wanted to lift them up: "Not that people will see that we have stood the test but that you will do what is right even though we may seem to have failed" (2 Cor. 13:7).

"It's about you," Paul was saying. "It's not about me."

LOVING THE ONES OVER US

Loving the one over us is love's deepest bow. In every case love means submission, but in the case of the person in authority over us, love means obedience. For those who hail from the City of Man, "You will not rule over me" is our natural battle cry—the "in your face" response of our first parents to God. It is not made easier when the people we are called to obey appear unworthy of the honor.

Paul addresses this matter in talking to slaves: "Obey your earthly masters with respect and fear, and with sincerity of heart, just as you would obey Christ. Obey them not only to win their favor when their eye is on you, but like slaves of Christ, doing the will of God from your heart" (Eph. 6:5–6). Peter clears up any possible objections by explaining that this applies "not only to those who are good and considerate, but also to those who are harsh" (1 Pet. 2:18).

The obedience of love we are called to render to authority must be sincere. We don't ingratiate ourselves in their presence, while disrespecting them behind their backs. This love is a genuine "fear" or recognition of actual authority. Not superiority, but authority. We obey sincerely, as those who are truly under the rule of another whose right it is to expect our obedience. We obey because it is the God-ordained way to love the people who are in authority over us—bosses, teachers, presidents, and parents.

Our resistance to authority breaks down when we realize that this submission is actually submission to Christ. The authority we recognize is his; the obedience we render is obedience to him. It becomes easier to obey because we don't want to disobey what is God's express will.

Obeying the men and women over us can be a profound delight when we realize it is actually Christ we are obeying. We do love him, after all, because he first loved us. In response, we long to have something to give him. "Were the whole realm of nature mine," an old hymn says, "that would be a present far too small." Yet Jesus told us what he wants: "If you love me, you will obey what I command. . . . My command is this: Love each other as I have loved you" (John 14:15; 15:12).

Jesus is saying something very serious, and we need to feel the gravitas of his commandment. "Do you love me?" "Do you truly love me?" "Do you truly love me?" Jesus asked Peter three times (see John 21). We gloss over, we ignore, we minimize his command to love—until we realize that Jesus equates this with *not* loving him.

When we begin to listen seriously, we find that Jesus is calling us into communion with himself—to a loving surrender to his authority in us that is the very substance of joy. Love of this kind is at the heart of the Godhead. Jesus rendered it to his Father when he abandoned himself to his Father's will, even to the point of death. Obedience is the deep delight God offered Adam when he gave him a command to obey in the Garden. It is the thing for which we were made.

LOVING THE LOST

Augustine, with impeccable logic, explains that loving God is our highest good. Therefore, as he put it, "He who loves God loves himself thereby. It follows that he must endeavor to get his neighbor to love God since he is ordered to love his neighbor as himself."[6]

Loving our neighbor means offering him Christ. The problem is that our neighbor, more often than not, doesn't want us to tell him about Jesus. In fact, he can get downright hostile about it. In certain times and places this anger will be expressed not just in ridicule and rejection but in loss of property, freedom, and even life. In order to love our neighbors, we must be willing to suffer.

Only Jesus can give us that kind of love. When we look at our neighbor with the eyes of compassion that Jesus gives us, our heart goes out to him. We believe all things for him, hope all things for him, and endure all things for him. In other words, we exercise a persevering faith on his behalf, seeing in him great potential through Christ. We want him as a brother.

Rather than respond to intimidation, we "sanctify Christ as Lord" (1 Pet. 3:15 NASB), which means we set Jesus apart as the one to be obeyed. We respond to him. He has given us his command to bring his message. On the basis of that authority we can even stand in the face of kings and rulers and testify to Jesus. This kind of fearless immunity to pleasing others comes from a deep recognition that Jesus is King of kings and Lord of lords, to whom every knee will bow. When Jesus gave his commission to the church to take the gospel to all people everywhere, he assured us that "all authority in heaven and on earth has been given to me" (Matt. 28:18) and that he would be with us in this endeavor to the very end of the age.

"Don't fear men," he said, "fear God" (see Matt. 10:26–28). And it is only by not fearing men that we can love them.

GETTING A LIFE

All this talk of dying and serving can get us carried away with the ego-gratifying idea of martyrdom. We can easily become enamored with the image of our noble self-sacrifice. Our love can quickly become condescending. The cure for this conceit is to remember from where we got life.

In the movie *Dead Man Walking,* the audience is presented with a despicable character—the lowest of the low, the one we all feel justified in hating. In fact, we feel guilty not hating him. He's on death row, convicted of raping and killing a teenage couple whom he and a buddy found parked one night in a lonely field. A nun is the only one who can stand him. She is assigned to be his spiritual advisor, and, as the movie unfolds, we watch her persevering love for him. He makes passes at her, demeans her, and tries to manipulate her. At one point he tells her he's going to heaven because he's been saved by Jesus, but his presumptuous, cocky sneer makes his statement appalling.

The nun rejects it. Her goal is to bring him to repentance. Patiently she asks him again and again if he's guilty, and he denies it again and again. But after awhile the audience knows he's lying because we see quick flashbacks of the horrifying scene. Finally, his appeals exhausted, the prisoner comes to the last half hour of his life. The specter of death gets through to him at last, and he repents with genuine remorse.

"You are a son of God," the nun tells him as he breaks down and cries.

At this point the guards come to take him to the room for lethal injection. A guard calls out, "Dead man walking," the traditional alert that the doomed convict is coming down the hall. The condemned man enters the designated room and looks through the window to where the parents of the murdered children are watching. "I am sorry for what I did," he tells them, "and I hope my death gives you some comfort." He is then strapped to the table with his arms outstretched to receive the needles. At one point, when he is raised up as the table rotates into position, he looks like Jesus on the cross.

This guilty man would not have had a life to offer if he hadn't repented and believed the gospel. His life was forfeit to justice. But as a son of God, the payment of his life had already been made by Jesus. He got his life back as a gift in order to offer it to others, humbled before them as the chief of sinners. Only because of the gospel was he able to identify with Christ in his death.

We are no different. We are all "dead men walking." We are each one the chief of sinners, for whom the opportunity to love as Christ loved, for the sake of Christ, is the highest privilege imaginable.

Loving involves a death of self-glory. Unfortunately, when we apply ourselves to loving, we run smack up against a wall of self-glory. We're like the man who went in for a psychiatric evaluation. When the psychiatrist asked him if he ever had unwanted thoughts, he answered, "Are there any other kind?"

We rake over the coals of our grievances and never find our hearts clear enough to love our enemies. We get caught up in thinking about the next rung in the City of Man, and loving seems like a waste of precious ladder-climbing time. Ulterior motives haunt us. We may even "prey" on people in the name of love, just to be able to boast about ourselves through them. The minute we do one simple loving thing, we find ourselves mulling it over with self-congratulatory pleasure.

All of this drives us back to the cross, where love took on our shame. The cross is what James calls the "law that gives freedom" (James 1:25; 2:12). It's like a mirror that exposes our natural selves and sets us free from any illusions of self-glory. At the same time, however, it sets us free from condemnation so we can follow Jesus in a throwing-caution-to-the-wind life of love. It shows us what that life looks like.

Simply put, the cross is the *means,* the *motive,* and the *measure* of City-of-God success.

Chapter 7
Living Deliberately

"Martha, Martha . . . you are worried and upset
about many things, but only one thing is needed."
JESUS TO MARTHA, LUKE 10:41

Slow food.

Imagine summer-red, vine-ripened tomatoes simmering in a pot with fresh herbs and garlic and sausage from the corner butcher. Imagine the aroma of homemade Italian bread baking in the oven, with creamy butter waiting on the table. Envision hand-kneaded dough coming out of the pasta cutter and being dropped into a pot of boiling water. The table is set with a red-checkered tablecloth and real cloth napkins, and there's a platter of antipasto as a centerpiece.

That's slow food.

In 1989, the International Movement for the Defense of the Right to Pleasure issued a slow-food manifesto declaring, "Our century, which began and has developed under the insignia of industrial civilization, first invented the machine and then took it as its life model. We are enslaved by speed and have all succumbed to the same insidious virus: Fast Life, which disrupts our habits, pervades the privacy of our homes and forces us to eat Fast Foods."[1]

The remedy, they decided, was slow food.

The snail—slow but delectable—is their symbol.

In a McDonald's world, the idea of slow food sounds like heaven. We long for a simpler, calmer life—like land-starved sailors catching a whiff of the delectable scents of a nearby island. Unfortunately, like those sailors, the storm just blows us right past and on out to sea. How can we have slow food? Who has time to prepare it? Who has time to eat it?

Then again, what kind of life is it when, as one executive confessed, she wakes to an alarm at 4:30 A.M. and, before leaving her bed, listens to her voice mail from the day before—usually averaging between twenty-five to forty messages? What has happened to us? What can we do about it?

According to author and speaker Dr. Richard Swenson, what has happened to us is progress.[2] Progress is that economic drive to do more and more, faster and faster. Through technology, progress has multiplied the complexity, speed, expectations, and demands that constitute life in the City of Man far beyond what we can manage. Communications alone have increased so rapidly that if operators had to handle the number of messages sent and received over the phone lines, one-third of the population of the United States would be needed to do the job. What we once thought would be time saving has simply increased our accessibility. The burden of responding to the number of people who can now reach us is overwhelming.

Choices—and the expectation that we analyze all our choices—are enough to swamp our feeble, mortal minds. Imagine a supermarket cereal aisle. A shopper is presented with more than two hundred options. Think of trying to analyze the price per unit of all these choices as well as keeping in mind the fact that you can get a rebate on this one, get one free if you buy that one, use the coupon in the little dispenser if you buy another one, or get a discount on this one if you remembered to bring the little card you slide through at the checkout counter. Then again, maybe the grocery store a mile away would be more economical. And what about nutrition? Are you eating low fat or high protein this week? On top of it all, your children are pressing for the cereal they've been hyped up to crave by the advertising they've seen on TV.

Swenson tells of a woman who said she was so busy that her idea of a vacation was going to the dentist. "I just can't wait to sit down in that chair," she said. For most of us, however, going to the dentist is just one more of the seemingly infinite number of things on our to-do list that weighs on us from the moment we get out of bed until we fall into bed again at night, exhausted and uneasy with guilt.

A SIMPLE REORIENTATION

After years of trying to squeeze it all in, the Swensons came to a screeching halt in 1982. Richard Swenson had been practicing medicine and teaching at the Wisconsin School of Medicine for twenty years. He and his wife had two young boys. They were active in their church. With all the meetings and activities, practically every moment of their lives was scheduled and they were always rushing from one thing to the next. Life had lost its margin.

"Everything had become a burden," Swenson says in retrospect, "medicine and patients, caring and serving." Richard was afflicted with migraines. Linda, his wife, found herself crying for no good reason. "Life was obviously out of control," Swenson remembers. "Joy dried up and blew away. Buoyancy sank. Enthusiasm evaporated. Rest was a theoretical concept.

My passion for medical practice shriveled to the size of a dehydrated pea."[3]

Swenson decided to look closely at the life of Jesus—someone who seems to have been able to live calmly and deliberately. People who read Swenson's books about the need for margin—for empty space in their lives—often make a new commitment to carve out a quieter, less hectic life for themselves. They may miss the point that the impetus behind his campaign is a singular realization that came from looking at how Jesus lived—a simple reorientation that motivated all the other changes.

FOCUSING ON PEOPLE

Jesus was not controlled by the agenda of the world system, Swenson realized. Jesus deliberately and purposefully resisted the flow of the world in order to live his life according to the will of God—which meant *giving his full attention to the person in front of him.*

"Jesus focused on the person standing in front of him at the time," says Swenson. "In my case, however, the person standing in front of me was often an obstacle to get around or over in order to get where I was going—even if that person was Linda or one of our sons."[4] Jesus, on the other hand, simply left many things undone in order to do the thing he was called to do. He did not heal everyone, but he gave the person he was with his undivided attention and love. Jesus seemed completely at peace about ignoring all the other demands and focusing on one single individual.

"When I finally learned these lessons about availability and prioritizing, life changed," Swenson explains. An observer tells of watching Swenson after a seminar when a long line of people were waiting to talk to him. Most people shook his hand, made a few comments, maybe got their copy of his book signed, and then moved on. One man, however, began to earnestly relate how his thirty-eight-year-old son had collapsed on the golf course the week before from the sheer exhaustion of marginless living. As the man told his story, he began to weep and was finally so overcome that Swenson had to physically support him. The thing that impressed the observer was that Swenson didn't try to hurry this man. He gave him his full attention in spite of the press of expectant and ultimately disappointed people lined up to talk to him.

God calls us to make people the priority. Once Richard and Linda Swenson realized that fact, they were able to uncomplicate their lives. With that simple, singular purpose, everything else fell into place. Cutting back on work hours; getting rest; limiting access; establishing emotional, physical, financial, and time reserves were all steps taken in order to answer the call of God upon their lives. The peace to resist the tide of progress and the disapproval of others came from the deep conviction that answering God's call was number one and that it necessitated having margins in their lives. The bottom line is following Jesus in his life of focused loving.

CHOOSING DELIBERATELY

If you glanced into the executive board room of Kaman Sciences in Colorado Springs, you'd never identify Lamar Allen, Ph.D., as the chief executive officer.[5] He doesn't exhibit that driving, impatient, type-A demeanor of most CEOs, and he spends more time listening than talking. When he speaks, he communicates with an unusual mixture of humility and quiet authority that make others strain to catch his every word. Under Allen's leadership, Kaman Sciences, a Defense Department think tank, has shown continuous double-digit growth, yet he breaks every stereotype of the successful executive.

In a word, Lamar is *calm.*

One of his employees describes it like this: "When he walks through the office, he isn't preoccupied and distracted. He stopped at my desk the day I returned to work after a miscarriage as if he had all the time in the world. His unhurried concentration on the person he is talking to communicates that he really cares. If there is a conflict in the office, both parties are always willing to submit to Lamar's judgment because he listens carefully to what each person has to say. You have confidence that he understands your point of view even if he doesn't decide in your favor. He is always fair."

In a schedule that includes multimillion dollar decisions as well as involvement in international defense concerns, Lamar chooses to shut the door on interruptions every Saturday in order to study the Scriptures and prepare a Sunday school lesson. He determinedly finds time to keep in touch with a few of the young adults who have been in his class by making regular calls every few months. When his grandchildren visit him at home, he's usually found in the middle of their games, laughing and having fun.

Living deliberately is the key to Lamar's peace. Simple-lifestyle advocates say that simple living is all about making deliberate choices out of a full awareness of why you're living life the way you are.

In Lamar's case that means making people the priority. He won't let life carry him helplessly along so that he never gets to the important stuff. This lifestyle has necessitated an unflinching, sometimes ruthless, elimination of other pressing demands. "The life of our Lord was, like our own, filled with a great tumultuous flow of events, yet he was able to focus on and accomplish the important things required of him," Lamar explains. "In John 17:4, the Lord says to the Father, 'I have brought you glory on earth by completing the work you gave me to do.' He didn't heal all the ill and afflicted, he didn't rid Israel of its Roman conquerors as he was so urgently expected to do, and no doubt the list of things he didn't do could go on and on." Jesus was immune to these pressures. He simply did the work the Father had given him to do.

"Our priority must always be people," Lamar explains. "We must be dedicated to discerning between what seems urgent and what is really important so we can do the things God intends for us to do."

SETTING LIMITS

Implicit in the idea of establishing margins and eliminating distractions is the very obvious realization that we *are* limited. We cannot do everything. We must determine what God is calling us to do and then not only be at peace leaving the rest to God but be filled with confidence and expectation about what he will do as we apply ourselves to our God-chosen territory.

In 1909 a young man named Jim Fraser stood in the doorway of a busy shop in a city near the frontier of Burma. Fraser had come there as a missionary with a special interest in the Lisu people—a large group of mountain clans who had never heard the gospel of Christ.

On this day he actually set eyes for the first time on four Lisu tribesmen who had come down from the mountains to transact business. Fraser's heart leapt at the sight of them as if they were long-lost friends. To his eyes they were beautiful because Fraser had narrowed the field. The kingdom of God is vast, but Fraser had defined his work within it. He knew which people God was calling him to specially love, and he was living purposefully and deliberately, concentrating on his territory. Fraser knew the need for limits.

"Think of the unlimited scope for the farmer in Canada," Fraser explained in a letter to his supporters back home. "There are literally millions of acres waiting to be cultivated.

The important thing is not the vastness of the territory, but how much of it is actually assigned to us. The Canadian government will make a grant of 160 acres to the farmer-emigrant, and no more. Why not more? Because they know very well that he cannot work any more. So they wisely limit him to an amount of land equal to his resources. . . . And he is not free to wander all over the prairie at his own sweet will and elect to settle down in any place he chooses. Even in regard to the position of his farm he must consult the Government."[6]

Fraser went on to explain that once our territory is assigned and the boundaries set, we can rest assured that as we apply ourselves to the task set before us, God will be at work.

LIVING PURPOSEFULLY

Simplicity comes when you become invested in what you do. You don't merely run into the store to buy a loaf of bread to cross it off the list; you thank God for providing your daily bread. Each thing you do is part of living in God's creation. You enter into situations where there are people to see and identify with—people God has placed in your path. When you smile and say thank-you to the clerk, you realize that he is a real person with joys and sorrows and burdens. Your smile is heartfelt. You stay alert to the "interruptions" in life—people like the poor beaten-up man the Samaritan came across. You recognize these as priorities.

"Live the moment" is a simple-lifestyle catchphrase. "Be where you are" is another. For the Christian, these reminders are loaded with significance. Each moment and place in which we find ourselves has been chosen for us by God.

We may not be called in the same way that Fraser was called to the Lisu (although we may be). But we can still know our assigned territory: coworkers, bosses, employees, the family we have, the people we come across, the students we teach, the individuals in the pew with us. They are the priority. They are our comrades, our fellow sinners, the ones of great value.

Augustine said, "All men are to be loved equally. But since you cannot do good to all, you are to pay special regard to those who, by the accidents of time, or place, or circumstance, are brought into closer connection with you. . . . You must take the matter as decided for you by a sort of lot, according as each man happens for the time being to be more closely connected with you."[7]

GIVING IT A REST

Fraser found peace in realizing that he not only couldn't do it all, he wasn't meant to do it all. This realization allowed him to live within the framework God had created and to accept his limits. He found he could not spend all day on his knees. He needed to get exercise. He needed to eat regularly. He needed to sleep. However he also needed to stay flexible and willing to suffer when divine interruptions came. Although much was left undone at the end of each day, he could give thanks because he knew that the frustrated goals and the setbacks were in God's hands.

When we have confidence that our day has been designed by God and that by choosing to give priority to the task of loving people we are pleasing him, then peace and simplicity come. We can approach life the way God approached Creation—one day at a time—a morning and an evening. At the end of each day, God looked at his work and pronounced it good. At the end of the week, after all the work was completed, God spent a full day resting.

God has divided life into manageable segments of time containing both labor and restorative rest. Every day has its own closure. Each week also has its own closure. This design was built into the world by God through the example of Creation. God created time—not as a tyrant ticking away, but so that everything would not happen at once. He divided it into parcels so that we wouldn't hurdle headlong from one thing to another. As the day closes, we can shut down. We don't have to rush ahead in our minds to tomorrow as we end today, fretting over all the things that aren't done. We can give it a rest.

We can pronounce our day good, regardless of what has been left undone, if we have redeemed the time, making the most of our opportunities to love. To the extent that we have not made the most of our opportunities—and this will always be the case—we can rest in the forgiveness of God and in the promise of a new day.

When we wake up to that new day, we mustn't hit the ground running as though life is one unbroken obligation. We have today. We ask for today's bread, and God promises he will provide—today. Our attention is free to be directed with anticipation to today's opportunity to seek first the kingdom of God. We invest ourselves in the opportunities as they present themselves—as to an adventure full of purpose and meaning. This is the day that the Lord has made. We can rejoice and be glad in it.

THE OBSTACLES TO SIMPLICITY

It sounds good, but why do we feel that the slow meal; the simple, quiet life; the ordered progression of work and rest; the making of others into the focus of life are all part of a dream beyond our reach? It seems that we face two serious obstacles: (1) Who's going to take care of things? and (2) What am I going to miss?

WHO'S GOING TO TAKE CARE OF THINGS?

Deep in our minds we instinctively realize that the fall of man intervened between the seventh day of Creation and us. Somehow we know that the rest we shared with God in the Garden was lost. We were cast out to fend for ourselves—to provide our sustenance through "painful toil," toil that is afflicted with "thorns and this-tles" (Gen. 3:17–18). We know that God condemned us to eat by the sweat of our brows. This is the state of things in the City of Man.

So when God restored the Sabbath in Exodus, he was effectively announcing that Redemption was coming. In telling the Israelites he would give them a double portion of manna on the sixth day so they could forget all about gathering and cooking and simply rest on the seventh day, he wasn't placing a burden on them. He was annulling the curse and giving them back the Sabbath! It was his gift to his redeemed people—a restoration of the rest that was lost. It was given on the basis of a promise of God's provision. The reason we can rest from our labors is that we're no longer striving to provide by the sweat of our brows. God not only gave miraculous food to his people to eat, he provided extra so they wouldn't have to fret about where the next meal was to come from on the seventh day.

The idea of real enjoyment of God's provision of rest is based on faith in the promise of God. We can be at peace about all the undone things and the problems we don't think we can solve because God has promised to provide for us. From the very beginning, the Sabbath was based on a promise that we're not fending for ourselves anymore—that God has stepped in to take care of us. It's no wonder God told Amos that Israel was like a basket of ripe figs—all ready for judgment—when their attitude toward the Sabbath was, "When will it be over so that we can go to market again?"

That market mentality has pushed most retailers into an open-seven-days-a-week schedule. But if you've ever tried to buy a chicken sandwich at the mall on Sunday, you know that Chick-fil-A is closed. This policy goes back to the beginning of the company.

"When Saturday came during our first week of business back in 1946," Truett Cathy, founder of Chick-fil-A, recalls, "Ben and I sank exhausted into a couple of chairs after the dinner crowd had thinned. Between the two of us, we had covered six twenty-four-hour shifts."[8]

"'What do you think, Truett?' my brother asked."

"'I think we ought to close tomorrow,' I replied."

"The thought of working around the clock on Sunday and then starting all over again on Monday was just too much. From then on, we told customers, 'We're open twenty-four hours a day, but not on Sunday.'"

Cathy has negotiated to have his restaurants closed on Sunday for more than fifty years since that first decision was made out of sheer exhaustion. The most common concern he's heard from his franchisees is, "Look at the business we're losing." In reality, they have usually generated more sales per square foot in six days than most similar restaurants do in seven.

Cathy's experience is just one example of the overwhelming body of evidence that God's promise is still good. We can take a rest without fear. God will provide.

Christians hold a variety of views on the necessity of keeping the Sabbath. For those who consider it a sacred day, there are different ideas about what that day is and what can be done on it. Paul says in Romans 14:5 that this was so even in the early church: "One man considers one day more sacred than another; another man considers every day alike."

Regardless of our convictions, however, we mustn't miss the bigger picture. The redemption heralded in the Sabbath law has been fulfilled by Jesus. It's no coincidence that Jesus performed so many healings on the Sabbath, infuriating the Pharisees who understood Sabbath keeping to be a work of righteousness. They didn't grasp the image—the Redeemer doing the work of Redemption that the human race, sick and paralyzed as we are, cannot do for ourselves. The Book of Hebrews tells us that the promised rest is like the promised land, which we enter when we believe the gospel and where we find rest from our independent struggle for life. When we believe it, we stretch ourselves out on the work of Jesus and relax.

We mustn't limit the idea of rest to one day or to the future consummation of the City of God. Jesus promises to give us rest now in very practical ways as we go through our circumstances, whatever they may be. You can rest in Jesus even while you're working. He knows you need a baby-sitter for Saturday night, a report finished by the deadline, taxes done that you've avoided, help with the overtightened lug nuts as you sit by the road with a flat tire the day after your road service expired. He understands the exigencies of modern life perfectly, and you can lean on him. Many Christians can testify that they often experience what Richard Swenson calls the "multiplying co-efficient" of God in their labors. He gets things done. He solves problems. He greases the wheels. And he infuses everything with peace.

A startling picture of the rest we can have in Jesus is Jesus himself asleep in the back of the boat during the storm. Paul echoes the image when—while on board a ship being destroyed by a hurricane—he calmly eats a meal. Paul was a prisoner of the Empire and was being taken to Rome for trial. The ship had been driven by a violent storm for fourteen days while the crew worked frantically "in constant suspense" (Acts 27:33). With the sea still raging, Paul reminded the men of what he had already told them— that God was in control. Then, Acts 27:35 says, "he took some bread and gave thanks to God in front of them all. Then he broke it and began to eat."

That was slow food eaten with deliberation even as the storm raged.

WHAT AM I GOING TO MISS?

Hebrews warns us against refusing the rest of God through fearful unbelief. Yet even when we're not afraid, we find it hard to slow down. Why is the mall so attractive? Why can't we just let the phone ring? Or turn off the television? The truth is that we are driven as much by desire as by fear. We don't want to miss out on the action. The reason progress continues to make economic sense is that we resonate to it in the depths of our souls. We want more and more faster and faster. We are in a perpetual state of grabbing for all we can get.

The City of Man is epitomized in the act of Eve reaching for the apple. She saw it. She wanted it. She took it. And Adam ate too—sealing our fate and determining the nature of humankind.

Theologians have called the essential driving force of man *concupiscence*—which simply means "beginning to desire." Concupiscence is not limited to unlawful sexual desires. It is any desire other than the desire for God. When Paul admits his inability to keep God's law against coveting in Romans 7, he bemoans the inescapable bent of his nature toward wanting whatever he sees.

To see it is to want it.

If it is denied to me, I want it even more.

Like the prodigal son, our innate approach to life is to get something for ourselves. Maslow took note of this in his study of human nature. People, he noticed, often don't feel a need for a thing until they become aware of it. He came to the conclusion that what he was calling *needs* might actually be more like *desires*. The compulsion within was created by the attraction without. What a perfect description of the fall of the human race. Eve saw that the apple was "good for food and pleasing to the eye, and also desirable for gaining wisdom" (Gen. 3:6).

What did she do? She took and ate.

The City of God, on the other hand, is epitomized by another act—Jesus taking the bread, giving thanks, and breaking it. "Take, eat," he said. "This is my body, broken for you." We receive this food like the prodigal son returning to his father. Our presumptions are gone. Our demanding hearts are humbled. We realize that our "grab" has brought us nothing but a pigsty. We know we don't deserve anything, and we dare not reach out our hands and presume to take anything. For returning prodigals, God pulls out all the stops. He puts on a feast, and he tells us with a shining face, "Take, eat."

COMMUNION WITH JESUS

The feast is communion with Jesus. What the City of Man lacks and can never find has been given to us abundantly in the City of God. In the last chapter of Ezekiel, God tells the prophet that the name of the City of God is "The LORD is there" (v. 35). The essence of the City of God is something we experience now. It is not primarily a place, but a communion with God.

God is everywhere, yet man cannot find him. But to the citizens of the City of God, he has manifested himself in Jesus. Communion with Jesus is at times a satisfying provision of sustenance, at other times a feast of delectable delights. At all times it is what gives us rest in the midst of the City of Man. When we go about our business in communion with him, all of life is "slow food"—purposefully, extravagantly savored. The simple peace we long for is not beyond our reach but right on the ship with us, even in the midst of the storm.

There can be little doubt that the communion we have with

Jesus is a mystery. We have the very mind of Christ. He shares himself with us internally. In the very depths of our minds and hearts he communicates his thoughts, his love, his way of seeing things—personally, one to one. This isn't generic classroom learning. Jesus, himself, gives us his full attention. He smiles on us and delights in us. He washes our feet as he continually presents himself alongside us as a satisfaction for our sin. He meets with us in the privacy of "the closet," where we go to escape the distractions of the world. He speaks to us directly through the Scriptures, making them shine with light and personal application. He reveals ourselves to us and brings us into the light concerning our sin. And as we repent, he shines the light of his communion and teaches us to love. In short, he gives us himself and everything he possesses.

Yet we meet him as much out in the world as we do by turning away from the world. We meet him in our work when it is "done for him." We meet him when we are in need and we present our requests to him. When we suffer, he suffers with us. And whatever we do for others, he receives it as done for himself.

We meet him in Creation by recognizing his love in the simple, good gifts he gives us. Joni Eareckson Tada explains: "When you realize you are among the least, the littlest, the last, and the lost, God becomes everything. To be caught up in his superior happiness is to see his love infused in and intertwined around everything. . . . To the contented person, the God-given token can be an hour of listening to Bach by the fireside. Sitting under a tree on a blustery day. Pulling over on the road to take in a kaleidoscope sunset."[9] Every good thing comes to us from the Father as a personal token of his individual love.

He is especially there in the middle of us when we fellowship as believers. He communicates himself to us through the many and varied gifts he has given to the Body. He stands with his face shining on us when we worship. Quintessential communion with Jesus is something we enjoy together when we partake of him in the Lord's Supper. The City of God is manifested when we come together as a church. Even when we're away from church, we are still acting communally as part of that City—bound together with our brothers and sisters on the basis of our shared communion with Jesus.

We really don't have to be afraid of missing anything after all. The City of God is truly where it's happening.

In the character of Mary Montague, novelist Elizabeth Goudge illustrates something of the depths and heights of what it means to have communion with Jesus. As a young girl, Mary dreamed glorious dreams of romance, heroism, and travel to exotic places. But on the occasion of her sister's wedding, reality hit her with devastating force. She was homely and deformed, and her family took it for granted that she was not presentable enough to be a bridesmaid. When she recovered from the death of her dreams, she began to pray about the options left to her. What should she do? "Love," was the answer she received. As she thought about this she wondered, *Could mere loving be a life's work?* Thus far, she realized, she hadn't loved any living thing except her cat.

Taking courage, she made a vow to the simplicity of loving and began to read her Bible—as "an engineer reads a blueprint and a traveler a map . . . with a profound concentration because her life depended on it. . . . It was then that the central figure of the Gospels, a historical figure whom she deeply revered and sought to imitate, began at rare intervals to flash out at her like live lightning from their pages, frightening her, turning the grave blueprint into a dazzle of reflected fire. Gradually she learned to see that her fear was not of the lightning itself but of what it showed her of the nature of love, for it dazzled behind the stark horror of Calvary."[10]

Mary Montague deliberately entered into a life of love in communion with Jesus, realizing that it required a death of her dreams of adventure. She chose a simple-lifestyle option: "I want to know Christ and the power of his resurrection and the fellowship of sharing in his sufferings" (Phil. 3:10). For Mary, that meant outwardly living a quiet, uneventful existence in her hometown, while under the surface she carried on a singular energetic adventure of love—praying continually for everyone she met.

Mary found the secret of slow-food, of making life a deliberately enjoyed feast through communion with Jesus.

Chapter 8
Weighing Truth

"If I am telling the truth, why don't you believe me?"
JESUS, JOHN 8:46

Nathanael was sitting in the shade of a fig tree, lost in his own thoughts. The fishing was over for the day; the catch, brought in and sold. His muscled back relaxed against the trunk of the tree, and his calloused hands hung limp as he enjoyed the cool afternoon breeze and the relief from the unrelenting heat of the sun. None of the other residents of the little town of Bethsaida, observing him under the fig tree, could possibly have known what was on Nathanael's mind. His thoughts were his own private preserve.

His reverie was broken when his friend Philip shook him by the shoulder. "We've found him," Philip said with breathless excitement. "We have found the one Moses wrote about in the Law, and about whom the prophets also wrote about—Jesus of Nazareth, the son of Joseph" (John 1:45).

Nathanael peered up into his friend's face, unmoved by Philip's enthusiasm. "Nazareth! Can anything good come from there?" he asked with his typical impassive skepticism (v. 46a). Philip didn't try to convince him. He had no answer to the problem of

Nazareth, an obscure and generally scorned little village. He simply said, "Come and see" (v. 46b).

Nathanael heaved himself up with a sigh, resigned to meeting this so-called messiah. With Nathanael following, Philip hurried down one narrow twisting street after another until they came to the outskirts of the town, where Jesus stood waiting. When he saw Nathanael, Jesus broke into a smile and said, "Here is a true Israelite, in whom there is nothing false" (v. 47).

"How do you know me?" Nathanael asked, not about to be taken in by flattery. But Jesus' answer rocked him to the core: "I saw you while you were still under the fig tree before Philip called you" (v. 48).

"Rabbi, you are the Son of God; you are the King of Israel," Nathanael declared (v. 49).

Jesus was not prone to giving words of praise to people. As the apostle John says, "He knew all men. He did not need man's testimony about man, for he knew what was in a man" (John 2:24–25). The fact was that Jesus had looked into Nathanael's heart while he was sitting under that fig tree and had seen nothing false, or as the New American Standard Bible puts it, "no guile." Nathanael, who thought he had been thinking in absolute privacy, recognized that Jesus had knowledge of him that no mere man could have.

In the midst of the City of Man, where falsehood and duplicity are the rule, Nathanael refreshed Jesus' heart—not because he was sinless but because he was interested in the truth. To us, Nathanael may look like a cynic, unwilling to believe anything. He may appear at first to be like Pilate, with his disillusioned question about truth. But Nathanael's skepticism was the opposite of Pilate's. He was so convinced of truth that he was immune to any other appeal. Forget putting Nathanael on any bandwagons.

Forget impressing him with anything. Nathanael was accepting no substitutes for the truth.

Once Nathanael found the truth, he automatically recognized its claim upon him. Once certain that Jesus was the Son of God, Nathanael's commitment was absolute. He was one of those who are "on the side of truth." Jesus told Pilate unequivocally, "I came into the world, to testify to the truth. Everyone on the side of truth listens to me" (John 18:37b).

The City of Man, on the other hand, is not on the side of truth.

THE CITY OF MAN'S BOX

In advising his apprentice on the art of tempting humans, C. S. Lewis's wily demon, Screwtape, pens this advice: "Your man has been accustomed, ever since he was a boy, to having a dozen incompatible philosophies dancing about together inside his head. He doesn't think of doctrines as primarily 'true' or 'false,' but as 'academic' or 'practical,' 'outworn' or 'contemporary,' 'conventional' or 'ruthless.'"[1]

Screwtape's advice wasn't new. The evil one has used this strategy from the beginning. In tempting Eve, he simply told a lie and then, without attempting to prove it, appealed to her on the level of self-interest. Eve responded, not by asking "Is this true?" but by asking "Does this serve my interests?" The logical absurdity of Satan's assertion, the evidence to the contrary, was a nonissue. She simply saw that the apple was "good for food and pleasing to the eye, and also desirable for gaining wisdom" (Gen. 3:6).

The City of Man has operated with a congenital disregard for truth ever since.

The phenomenon of public support for President Clinton during the Monica Lewinsky drama is an example. There seemed to be a tacit agreement between the public and Mr. Clinton in which he was saying, "I really want you to believe in me," and the public was saying, "We really want to believe in you." Most people didn't seem to care whether there was reality behind Clinton's denials. "What is true?" simply wasn't the issue.

This was made even more apparent by the public's indifference when the discrepancy between reality and Mr. Clinton's words came to light. The prosecutors, who assumed that proving Clinton's deception would create indignation in the public, found out that "What is true?" really isn't the salient question in the City of Man. We've always been willing to believe in an idol if it serves our ends.

In Isaiah 44, God talks about how patently absurd it is to worship something that is obviously the construction of man. "He . . . fashions a god and worships it," God says. "He prays to it and says, 'Save me; you are my god'" (vv. 15, 17). We manufacture something and then we choose to believe in it—to see it as "true" because it meets our needs.

Idols are not so much physical objects as internal beliefs. The City of Man chooses its idolatrous beliefs as if it were shopping at a supermarket, without ever stopping to ask, "Is this reality?" "Is this true?" According to God, we have even lost the capacity to discern the obvious fact that the thing we believe in is false. It isn't even a question we ask.

THINKING OUTSIDE THE BOX

Harriet Segal had fashioned a "truth" that served her well.[2] Although she and her husband, Richard, are Jewish, she had never taken faith in God seriously, and as a young adult she had decided to be an atheist. Being a person who does not handle ambiguity well, she chose simply to eliminate the possibility of any existence beyond the material world. In Harriet's mind lurked the unexamined assumption that one truth was as good as another since truth was not absolute, but functional and subject to invention.

Richard, on the other hand, liked to leave his options open. He had toyed with the idea that Jesus was Messiah since his college roommate had presented him with the gospel. Richard had sensed "something different" about his roommate and had been on the lookout for Christians ever since. Whenever he met someone who had that "something different" quality, he would find out if they were Christians, and, remarkably, they almost always were. Twenty-eight years later, Richard was convinced that Jesus was indeed Messiah. Still Richard remained like someone sitting on the porch of a house who never really considers going in.

One day, following a discussion with Richard about Christianity, Harriet's patience was so depleted she suggested they ask Jesus for proof of his existence and settle the issue once and for all. Richard boldly asserted that he believed Jesus would prove himself. "In fact," he said, "I believe Jesus will send someone to help Amy."

Their daughter, Amy, had been struggling at Princeton as she searched for the meaning of life. Since Harriet had been unable to solve Amy's problem on the practical level where she normally operated, she agreed to ask this hypothetical "Jesus" to help, but she insisted that they set a deadline—March 1—three months away. They also agreed not to tell Amy.

Harriet recalls, "I thought it might happen because I had recently come to accept the possibility of mind control, not as something supernatural, but as something that was perhaps part of the natural order that we simply didn't understand yet. I thought maybe Richard could make this happen simply because he believed it so implicitly. On February 21 I asked him if he needed more time, but he assured me that Jesus would do it."

The morning of March 1, Amy called and said, "Mom, last night, at a quarter to twelve, a Christian friend, a guy I've known for awhile, knocked on my door. We talked about Jesus, and I am going to consider Christianity."

Isn't that odd, Harriet thought.

She still wasn't convinced, but she had crossed a line. It had become possible to her that there was what Francis Schaeffer called "true truth"—not a subjective reality that she chose herself, but an objective reality that, by virtue of its being true, would have a claim on her life.

She dug out a little evangelistic book that Richard had acquired years ago. The book was written for Jewish people and focused on the Old Testament prophecies fulfilled by Jesus. Within a few hours Harriet had prayed the prayer of faith and commitment in the back of the book. A few days later, Richard also "went in."

By God's grace, Harriet and Richard were enabled to break out of the City of Man's "box." Apart from God's revelation, our thinking has limited horizons. We can use our reasoning abilities to think "inside the box," but we are inevitably predisposed against considering a reality outside the box. Logic stops at the boundaries of the City of Man. Beyond that line, things seem confused and cloudy.

What is this box? In the City of Man, everything is considered as though man is at the center. Man is the biggest thing. Man is the judge of all things. Man approaches the question of God from the point of view of a judge considering the merits of God's case. Every individual is encouraged to put "self" in the judgment seat. Each of us feels empowered with the authority to choose our reality.

When Paul said in Romans 1 that man suppresses the knowledge of God, he didn't mean that no one professes belief in God within the City of Man. He meant that man innately represses the reality that he is not at the center of the universe, that there is a true and living God at the center who judges and rules. So, when man considers ultimate questions, he does so with an instinctive predisposition not to consider anything as ultimate. He relegates God to the murky unknowable regions outside the box so he doesn't have to deal with him. With God out of the picture, man is the biggest thing. He can go about his business as he pleases. He can choose his belief system.

When Paul went to Athens, he found the City of Man in full throttle. There were idols everywhere. Up on Mars Hill, man was sitting as judge, weighing the newest philosophies without any intention of settling the issue of ultimate truth because that would mean relinquishing the judgment seat. Paul moved into their box with the proclamation that God is central. He is the one in whom their very existence rested, and his message to them through Paul had the full authority of true truth. Not hypothetical truth, but reality. Not something for them to judge and consider, but a message declaring that God was judging and considering them!

Paul used their idol "TO AN UNKNOWN GOD" (Acts 17:23) as his point of departure. "You have used your reason to arrive at a true conclusion. There is a God you do not know. Now I am going to make him known to you." But the City of Man does not want to know him. It cannot even consider the possibility of the true and living God because then the entire premise on which the City of Man has been built would be overthrown. The world would be seen as it actually is—a God-centered reality—and the man-centered illusion would be shattered.

The pride of man and his self-chosen darkness were expressed in the sneer the Athenians gave to Paul's testimony about the Resurrection. This was not rational disbelief. It was the mind of man closed against the put-down of believing in a real God who acts in history. The City of Man doesn't genuinely ask the question

"What is truth?" because the very idea of authoritative truth is a threat to its glory.

Even so, some in Athens listened to the gospel and believed. A few were called out from the City of Man into the City of God.

THINKING INSIDE THE BOX

The wealthy Philadelphia industrialist Albert C. Barnes was a contemporary of John Dewey and, like Dewey, was a believer in the scientific method. There is an integrity about the scientific method that comes from its commitment to making unbiased observations and drawing logical conclusions—in other words, to identifying reality. Barnes applied the scientific method to the study of aesthetics. He believed that really good works of art could be identified by objective observation. He rejected the subjective "I don't know what's good; I just know what I like" approach to art and began trying to determine what good works of art from all the different historical periods have in common. He concluded that there were certain qualities that exist objectively in the world—gentleness, delicacy, power, mystery, cheerfulness, drama, variety, and so forth—and that humanity is universally constituted to perceive them and respond with aesthetic appreciation. The artist is primarily a discoverer who has aesthetic insight into the objective world and who interprets that reality in a way that makes it apparent to others.

Barnes began to collect works of art that illustrated his conclusions. He identified as "good" the works of many Europeans who were only beginning to be known—artists like Degas, Renoir, and Matisse. Rejecting the pretensions of the Philadelphia art community, he hung his collection in his factory, and when his uneducated workers showed an interest, he shortened the work day and turned the factory into an art institute. In 1994, the Barnes collection went on world tour and broke attendance records in almost every major city.

Barnes's ability to identify art that has since been universally accepted as "true art" is a profound verification that the world is not an arbitrary place. Logically, such objective evidence of a design in nature would lead to the conclusion that there is a Designer. But Barnes, like Dewey and others from their school, refused to think outside the box. Their integrity had its limits. They were content to hold certain ideals as absolute while refusing to see that no value can be absolute in an uncreated, accidental world.

As Screwtape put it, humankind is comfortable having a "dozen incompatible philosophies dancing about together inside their heads." We live in an irrational, human-centered world where logical inconsistencies are the norm because God is not given glory.

THE INVASION OF GLORY

When the glory of God invades our lives through the gospel, it reorders our entire perspective. Like Nathanael, we realize that the one we are seeking is seeking us. He is the Knower. He is the Seer. He is the Judge. The lie that was our refuge is exposed, and we realize that he offers us the only real refuge.

The center of the universe shifts.

The Field Museum in Chicago recently opened an "Underground Adventure" that allows you to view the world from a few inches below the earth's surface. They've designed an environment where you can examine plant roots, follow the trail of a mole, or encounter an earwig big enough to do some real damage. The larger-than-life models create the illusion that you've shrunk to 1/100 of your normal size.

God's glory does the same kind of thing, but it is no illusion. God's glory brings a sane reality. By bringing to light how things really are, we get a proper sense of proportion. God is great. All glory, honor, and power are his.

Yet we live acknowledging him in the midst of a city that does not acknowledge him. We live in the light of a reality that the City of Man does not get. Whether it's *Time* magazine or the latest sitcom, secular media reads the world from a perspective that assigns no significance to Christ and his saving work.

In the midst of this kind of propaganda, citizens of the City of God must live as aliens. We must consistently "see through" the City of Man in order to give weight to the truth and walk in the light. We must take every thought captive to make it obedient to Christ, not only for the sake of God's glory, but for the sake of those trapped in the box to whom we wish to offer a bold testimony to the truth. When King Agrippa asked if Paul thought he could persuade him to become a Christian, Paul's answer was a heartfelt, "I pray God that not only you but all who are listening to me today may become what I am, except for these chains" (Acts 26:29).

How was Paul different from King Agrippa and his friends, Governor and Mrs. Festus? Paul had seen the light of the glory of God. But God's glory was not merely a generic fact. Paul had seen the glory of God *in the face of Christ*.

God has called a halt to the times of "ignorance," as Paul said when he witnessed to the Athenians (Acts 17:30). He has broken into the box with an authoritative call to acknowledge the true and living God. But the thing that pierces the darkness, that opens up the box, is the Son of God crucified for the sins of the unbelieving world.

The glory of God is something sinful man cannot handle. It drives us deeper into darkness, fleeing exposure. Yet the death of Jesus calls us out into the light—exposed, but deeply loved and forgiven. From then on living in the City of Man as faithful citizens of the City of God simply requires walking in the light of the reality of the gospel.

WALKING IN THE LIGHT

Integrity is just another word for walking in the light. It means that nothing is swept under the rug. Everything is exposed to the light of truth so there's a consistency that runs through all of life. Thought, word, and deed are cut from the same cloth, and truth prevails at any cost.

TRUTH AND BUSINESS

One of the basic realities implicit in the gospel is God's justice. The fact that we've been forgiven for all the things we've done in darkness shouldn't lead to presumption. Rather, seeing the cost that the Son of God paid makes justice even more awesome. God is serious about this stuff. He calls us to live in the light, loving truth in every arena of life.

But it's not easy. Nowhere are the pressures to live by the premises of the City of Man stronger than in the marketplace. Choosing to walk in the light can cost you dearly in the world of business.

Take the Meloons for example. As believers, they didn't expect God to provide them with health and wealth. Nonetheless, their family's small boat business, Correct Craft, was riding a wave of optimism and prosperity in the booming 1950s. During WWII, the company had met a seemingly unmeetable deadline, building more than four hundred boats in time for the army to cross the Rhine into Germany. This reputation for reliability helped land a government contract for more than three thousand boats in 1957.

Production was underway when the chief of the three-man government inspection team made it clear that an under-the-table payoff was expected—even though the contract clearly said no gratuities. "We couldn't even give an inspector a Coca-Cola or a cup of coffee," Ralph recalls.[3]

The Meloons didn't pick up on the inspector's hint, and they soon felt the repercussions. Before that meeting, two thousand boats had been produced and accepted. After the meeting, the inspection team started finding "flaws," and by the end of the year, six hundred rejected boats lay in the Meloons' warehouse.

More than once during that long, slow, unfair process, the Meloons were tempted to pay the bribe. It didn't amount to much, while the losses, on the other hand, were going to be fatal. Unable to sleep one night, W. O. Meloon got up and read his Bible. The following words seemed to glow: "Trust in the Lord with all your heart." The reality of God's nearness began to outweigh the fear. Two things seemed obvious to W. O. First, integrity matters to God. He hates bribes, rigged scales, deals behind the scenes, and everything that is dishonest and hidden. Second, they could trust God. He was a rock, and they could hide in him as long as the storm raged.

After everything was said and done, Correct Craft owed a half million dollars to 228 creditors, and the Meloons took chapter 11 bankruptcy. Their struggle to live with integrity was just starting. For years they worked to build back the company and repay their debts. Ralph and Betty Meloon lived in a tent as they traveled the Midwest, developing new markets for their product. With fifty thousand dollars of debt left in 1984, Correct Craft sponsored a bass-fishing team to promote their boat, the Bass Nautique. Correct Craft and the team agreed to split the prize if they won.

They won. One half of the one-hundred-thousand-dollar prize money paid the last of the Meloons' debt. They were finally in the clear, and today Correct Craft is a worldwide company offering a witness to the gospel with every boat they sell.

TRUTH AND POLITICS

The political arena is perhaps equal to the marketplace in challenges to integrity. Florida congressman Charles Canady says that politics seems to attract individuals with strong egos. "Shy and retiring types don't usually seek office," he says with a smile. "Politics draws people who, more than most, love the sound of their own voices."[4]

As a Christian, Canady has given the matter of integrity a lot of thought. He says:

The only way it's possible to stay focused on the things that are truly important is to understand something that a theologian, John Murray, said many years ago. He wrote that "the claims of truth are paramount." It's a principle that applies in every realm of life. It certainly applies in politics. In politics, truth is challenged on an ongoing basis, and respect for truth is hard to find.

To serve in politics and to maintain allegiance to the Kingdom of God, to the eternal city, in the midst of that service, the critical requirement is to remember that the claims of truth are paramount—always. Whenever political expedience moves contrary to the claims of truth, that's when the answer to expediency must be "No."

Of course, politics is based on compromise because politics means gathering together people with different goals and different desires and different objectives and trying to reach common ground. In order to do that, everybody has to give up something. In politics you cannot have everything exactly the way you want it.

The key is this: In the process of compromise, you can't lose sight of the fact that "the claims of truth are paramount," and you can't engage in compromise that sacrifices the truth.

> Sometimes people will disagree about whether a
> compromise has sacrificed the truth or whether it
> is just the best that can be done given the practi-
> cal constraints that exist. But the struggle to place
> truth as the paramount consideration must be
> maintained.

Canady was one of the House trial managers who prosecuted
President Clinton in the U.S. Senate. This was not an issue for
compromise, in his opinion. As far as he and his fellow managers
were concerned, the rule of law was threatened. But for Canady,
the issue went beyond the pragmatic implications for our system
of government. As a Christian, he believes that justice in the City
of Man must mirror the unflinching integrity of God's justice.
From Canady's perspective when the President was acquitted, justice and truth lost the day.

His consolation?

"I know that truth will prevail in the long run," he says. "I
don't worry about the ultimate victory of truth. It's a disappointment when, for the moment, it seems that truth is not honored,
but as we experience these things, it's just a reminder of the day
when all the injustice will be set right and all the falsehood will be
burned away by the brilliant light of truth. That day will come."

TRUTH AND RELATIONSHIPS

Paul assured the Corinthians that his heart was wide open to
them. He told the Thessalonians that he wasn't putting on a mask
to cover greed. At Galatia he called Peter down for his hypocrisy.

Christian relationships, according to Paul, require a radical
kind of integrity that only comes when the heart is open to God.
Duplicity comes from trying to get praise from men. Paul didn't
care whether anyone approved of him. He wanted to be laid bare
by the light of truth, and if his heart was dark, he wanted the light

to shine in and expose and purify it. He knew what it was like to be so self-deceived that you can approve of yourself while, in God's eyes, you are doing the darkest evil. Paul was through with all that. The exposure he experienced on the road to Damascus was like the dawning of the sun. He wanted to keep walking in the light, exposed down to the foundations of his soul.

Only the gospel can produce that kind of integrity.

Westminster Theological Seminary professor Dr. C. John Miller used to tell two stories on himself to illustrate the difference the gospel can make.

One day he was driving past a local hamburger stand when he did a sharp U-turn. Several teenaged boys were ridiculing an elderly woman, and Dr. Miller was incensed. He pulled into the parking lot, jumped out of his car, and started railing at the teenagers about the fifth commandment. After he began to wind down, he told them he expected to see them all in church the next Sunday. "The trouble," Dr. Miller said, "was that I had no joy to share with them. I was right in my indignation about their sin, but I had no corresponding indignation about my own sin, so the Gospel had become meaningless to me."[5]

A few years later Dr. Miller had another experience at another hamburger drive-in where the local teenaged toughs hung out. When he arrived that evening, he asked the young men to gather around, and he introduced himself to them. Then he began to share the gospel, beginning with God's indignation for sin, but following with the amazing substitution that God made when he poured out his indignation on his Son instead. One young man, the leader of the group, reminded Dr. Miller that he had hitched a ride with him a few weeks earlier and had been given a tract explaining the gospel.

"I've been thinking about it," he said. "I've tried to call you, but your daughter keeps hanging up on me." A few weeks later, Bob

Heppe repented and believed the gospel. He stopped dealing heroin and spent two years paying back everything he had stolen. Now he is a missionary to West Asians in London.

What made the difference in Dr. Miller?

Radical honesty. "Truth in the inner parts," as Psalm 51:6 puts it. Dr. Miller had started living a life of ongoing repentance leading to an ongoing renewal of joy in the gospel.

"The union of compassion and integrity is found in the man who repents. . . . The man with a broken and contrite heart has learned something about love and honesty before God. No longer is he a crusader driven by a proud human emptiness," Dr. Miller explains.

"True, as he grows in holiness he senses the acute difference between himself and the world. . . . Unrepentant men are still in darkness. The repentant is now in God's kingdom. But he also knows that he has a great deal in common with all men. Although he has been cleansed by the precious blood of Christ, he is still a man and he is also a sinner. As his repentance deepens, he learns to see other men compassionately.

"He knows that God broke through his own thick shell, and that all good in himself originated with a sovereign invasion from without. . . . The aim of it all is to get a loving integrity which comes only from a life lived in the presence of God."

Chapter 9

Taking Action

"Everyone who hears these words of Mine,
and acts upon them, may be compared to a wise man,
who built his house upon the rock."
JESUS, MATTHEW 7:24 NASB

When missionaries come home on furlough they all experience the same thing: they see things with different eyes. To some extent they've gained the perspective of a foreigner. From this new point of view, their home culture can sometimes look shocking.

"When I first came home from the field," one missionary reports, "I was rocked by the affluence. But after a while I got acclimated, and I began to feel the American Dream like a siren's call. I felt like I was missing out on life. I remember going to spend the weekend at the home of some relatives. They had all kinds of toys. First, we rode on the jet skis. When we got tired of that, we rode on the motorcycles. And when we were worn out from recreating, we watched movies on the big-screen TV. That night when I went to bed, I thought to myself, *I can't give any of this stuff to my family.* I felt like a fool—like someone who was giving up the real stuff to pursue some idealistic dream. The temptation to chuck it all and come home to start building a life of possessions was very powerful."

This missionary felt himself being pulled into the City of Man. He had to fight to maintain the perspective he had when he first returned from the mission field. The City of Man was casting a spell over him, and he was caught in a battle of resistance that we are all called to fight.

We are like fish who have been immersed in the water so long we aren't even aware of it anymore. We need to be "fish out of water"—people who can see the City of Man with the fresh perspective of the City of God and then live that way. The fact is, we can most effectively resist the attractions of the City of Man by *taking action in a contrary direction*. The battle is won through decisive moves in the direction of the City of God.

D. Martyn Lloyd-Jones was a Welshman who exhibited great promise early in life. His academic achievements had earned him distinction. His pursuit of a career in medicine took him to the pinnacle of that arena in the United Kingdom—acceptance into Saint Bartholomew's Hospital in London.

"Bart's doctors, like graduates of Trinity College, Cambridge, acquire a feeling that membership in their institution alone is enough to set them somewhat apart, that they are not like other men." They have a "consciousness of effortless superiority."[1]

Lloyd-Jones was not only accepted as a student in the company of this elite group, but his examinations at the end of that time earned him degrees with distinction and the attention of Sir Thomas Horder, Bart's most brilliant physician.

Horder broke the precedent of only appointing physicians from his own firm and appointed Lloyd-Jones as his junior house physician. After that Martyn became Horder's chief clinical assistant, treating the celebrities and national figures of London. Horder also began including Lloyd-Jones in the rarefied circle of his social connections. When he took his postgraduate examination for membership in the Royal College of Physicians in April 1925, his reputation in the medical world was already eminent, and his place in the upper echelon of London society was secure.

Running parallel to these years of medical training was an awakening in Lloyd-Jones's heart. Already a believer, he began to "see through" the glory of the City of Man. In 1923, as he reclassified Horders' case histories, he was amazed to realize that 70 percent of these upper-class patients were diagnosed with "eats too much," or "drinks too much." This medical index became to him like Ezekiel's vision of a valley of dry bones.

In contrast, he saw the glory of the cross of Christ in a new and overwhelming way.

The more he moved among the "party guests" of the City of Man, the more hollow it seemed. The cross loomed large as the only hope for the human race. And yet, it also seemed impossible to extricate himself from it all, even when he was sure God was calling him to preach the gospel. Whenever he contemplated such a move, he felt the overpowering judgment of the City of Man saying, "You fool." One evening in his study he was deeply moved by the love of God expressed in the death of Christ. Yet his attachment to the glory of the City of Man still had a grip on him. "It was a very great struggle," he said in retrospect. "I literally lost over 20 pounds."[2]

The struggle was finally decided in favor of the City of God one evening in 1926. Lloyd-Jones had spent the evening in the company of well-to-do friends at the theater, and as they emerged into the blare and glare of London's Leicester Square, a Salvation Army band came along playing hymns.

Martyn said in later years, "I knew these were my people. I have never forgotten it. There is a theme in Wagner's opera, *Tannhauser*, the two pulls—the pulls of the world and the chorus of the pilgrims—and the contrast between the two. I have very often thought of it. I know exactly what it means. I suppose I had enjoyed the play. When I heard this band and the hymns I said, 'These are my people, these are the people I belong to, and I'm going to belong to them.'"³ By the following year, Lloyd-Jones had announced he was leaving medicine to go into the ministry.

BREAKING THE CITY OF MAN'S SPELL

C. S. Lewis's children's stories often contain profound truths. In *The Silver Chair*, Jill and Eustace and the marshwiggle, Puddleglum, go down to the underlands on a quest to free the prince of Narnia from an evil serpent who has him imprisoned. All through the adventure the three are called to "see through" things as they appear and to act on Aslan's words alone. More than once they're deceived by the way things seem. The lure of comfort and ease almost puts them on the menu at a giant's feast. Finally they come to the prince and find, to their dismay, that he has been deceived as well. The serpent has taken the form of a beautiful queen whose enchanting words seem irresistibly reasonable. She has told the prince that he falls into a fit of madness at a certain time every day. During that time he must be chained to a silver chair.

In reality this is the only time when the prince is "in his right mind"—when he remembers who he is, that the overworld is his true home, and that the queen is evil. But before Puddleglum and the children can free the prince, the queen begins to enchant *them* as well. She tells them over and over that there is no overworld, that it is only a dream.

Finally Puddleglum musters his last measure of resolve and walks over to the fireplace and stamps his foot on the embers. The smell of burnt marshwiggle breaks the spell. Everyone snaps out of it and does battle with the queen, who has assumed her true form. They slay the serpent, free the prince, and save Narnia. Puddleglum tells the children that there's nothing like a little pain to dispel the effects of an evil spell.

When we do battle against the alluring illusions of the City of Man, we, too, need to take decisive action—maybe even feel a little pain. It's the best way to break the spell of the world. There are always two strains of music calling to us, but at times the siren call of the City of Man overwhelms the pilgrim's chorus. It cost Lloyd-Jones blood, sweat, and tears to break away and join up with the pilgrims.

Breaking away doesn't always mean becoming a missionary or a minister, but it *does* mean making choices. It means setting our course through decisive action.

THE FOCUS OF FAITH

From Scripture it's pretty clear that our whole way of looking at things, valuing things, and making choices should be shaped by the cross and the return of Jesus. We live between them in what the Bible calls "the last days." Having a City-of-God perspective means seeing everything in light of these nonpareil events. If we give weight and glory to these two actions of God, we will stay in "our right minds." Seeing life apart from the cross and the return of Jesus is a lie—the operating delusion of the City of Man.

A NEW SET OF DESIRES

Seeing the cross of Jesus is a breathtaking, transforming experience. As one theologian put it, all of the vastness of the universe is nothing but a stage to display the glory of the cross. From the City of Man's perspective, all the years from the time when Adam and Eve made their choices seem to be just one, unchanging panorama—with God, if he exists, being passive and removed. In reality, however, God has been actively involved, sustaining the world and causing the rain to fall and the sun to shine and order to prevail over chaos. He has been restraining the outworking of sin in the human race and restraining his judgment against humanity.

Why? Because he so loved the world.

How much? Enough to send his Son to take the weight of judgment upon himself. Breathtaking!

In the Song of Songs, the lover knocks at the door of the bedroom of his beloved and she tells him to go away; she can't be bothered to get up and unlatch the door. She's already in bed, and she's washed her feet. If she has to walk all the way across the floor to let him in, she'll get her feet dirty. What does the lover do? He reaches in through the opening to unlatch the door, and that awakens love for him in the beloved's heart. But when she runs to the door, he's gone. She wanders through the streets looking for him. She also warns the other maidens: "Do not . . . awaken love until it so desires" (3:5b).

The cross is the Beloved's hand reaching through the door.

Jesus desired us that much. When we wouldn't have given two cents for him, when we were his enemies, he laid down his life for us. His pursuing love awakens a passionate desire for him in our souls.

Yet he is gone. We love him and know him in the her and now, but we also feel his absence intensely. All our desires are to be with him. We live in anticipation of seeing him face to face. And we will! He will return. On *That Day* as the Bible calls it, Jesus will come again, and we will be with him forever in face-to-face adoration.

Revelation 21 describes the City of God as a bride prepared for her husband. The day of Christ's return will be the consummation of our desires and his. "To have found God and still to pursue Him is the soul's paradox of love," says A. W. Tozer.[4] To know that our love will be fully satisfied on That Day is life's transforming realization. Everything else pales by comparison.

As Augustine said, the "two cities have been formed by two loves."[5] One by a love for all that the City of Man has to offer and one by a love for God. There is a mutual exclusiveness about these two loves. God wants us to have "singleness of heart" (Col. 3:22 RSV); to love and desire only one thing; to say, like David, "Whom have I in heaven but you? / And earth has nothing I desire besides you" (Ps. 73:25). He wants us to love the Lord our God with all our heart, soul, mind, and strength.

Singleness of love gives us a singleness of purpose: "We make it our goal to please him," Paul says (2 Cor. 5:9). Hearing him say "Well done" is the great reward of a heart that loves the Lord Jesus. It gives us a *Who cares?* kind of attitude about the glory of the City of Man. *Who cares?* when we have Jesus and have been promised on That Day a reward of glory for having loved the City of God rather than the City of Man.

The incentives the Bible offers wouldn't appeal to an unredeemed citizen of the City of Man. They aren't self-serving in a way that satisfies the desire for personal glory. They are totally oriented to Jesus. Listen to what C. S. Lewis said in his essay entitled "The Weight of Glory": "It is promised, firstly, that we shall be with Christ; secondly, that we shall be like Him; thirdly, with an enormous wealth of imagery, that we shall have 'glory'; fourthly, that we shall, in some sense, be fed or feasted or entertained; and finally, that we shall have some sort of official position in the universe—ruling."[6]

All of these realities are true in some measure while we live by faith in the City of Man, but the foretaste only creates a greater hunger for the fullness. What's more, all of these realities are oriented to Jesus. If we don't desire him, if he isn't the object of our affections, then these rewards will sound insipid—tasteless. If we are hungry and thirsty for him, however, they will motivate us to live with all our energies focused on That Day.

"To please God," Lewis says, ". . . to be a real ingredient in the divine happiness . . . to be loved by God, not merely pitied, but delighted in as an artist delights in his work or a father in a son— it seems impossible, a weight or burden of glory which our thoughts can hardly sustain. But so it is."

In nearly every letter of the New Testament we find some variation on this theme: Make the hope of That Day the transforming motivator of your life. Shake off the constraints, throw caution to wind, wake up, and live for That Day, the day of the City of God. Martin Luther said there were only two days on his calendar: "Today" and "That Day."8

The key, according to Hebrews 11:1, is to have confidence in the things hoped for and certainty of the things not seen—to believe that the City of God will be made manifest, to have the eyes of our hearts enlightened to see the unseen things, to have the things hoped for gain weight and reality in our estimation. Then we need to act on it.

A NEW SET OF FEARS

The cross and the return of Jesus give us not only new desires but a fresh set of fears as well—good healthy fears that free us from the anxieties we often experience in the City of Man.

We need to understand that the cross speaks a warning as well as a welcome to the world.

When Peter preached to the Jews in Jerusalem and told them that the man they had crucified had been raised from the dead and confirmed by the resurrection to be both Lord and Messiah, the people were full of the fear of God. But it wasn't only the Jewish leaders in partnership with Pilate who crucified the Lord. Paul says, "None of the rulers of this age understood it [i.e., the wisdom of the cross], for if they had, they would not have crucified the Lord of glory" (1 Cor. 2:8).

The Lord of Glory was put to death by the City of Man.

But God raised the Son from the dead and seated him above every authority in heaven and on earth. And the Son will return suddenly, at an unknown time, to judge the world.

Look at Psalm 2: "I have installed my King on Zion, my holy hill," God says to the City of Man (v. 6). And then the psalmist says, "Be warned, . . . / Kiss the Son, . . . / for his wrath can flare up in a moment" (vv. 10, 12).

The appalling specter of the Son of God nailed to a cross inspires fear in anyone with an ounce of sense. When the Jews realized what they had done, they cried out to Peter, "What shall we do?" And he told them, "Repent and be baptized, every one of you, in the name of Jesus Christ for the forgiveness of your sins" (Acts 2:38). In other words, "Find a safe haven in the very One you put to death." Psalm 2 ends with the same excellent advice, "Blessed are all who take refuge in him" (v. 12b).

The cross is a haven from the judgment that is coming upon the world on That Day. But even believers are encouraged to let That Day inspire a wholesome fear—not of judgment, but of the passing over of judgment. There is safety in the Son, but safety from a terrible time of exposure and retribution, when even believers will be either ashamed or covered in glory depending on how they have built upon the foundation of Christ.

On That Day everything hidden will be made manifest. The truth will be plainly revealed. There will only be one opinion on That Day—God's opinion—and every knee will bow in acknowledgment that his judgments are just. Some will bow with joy;

some, with joy mixed with shame and regret; others, with terror. Every heart will be exposed. The glory of the City of Man will be shown up for exactly what it is, and those who have "clothed" themselves with it will be found naked.

The key, again, is believing it.

When the reality of judgment sinks in, we find that our other anxieties and fears shrivel up and blow away. Whatever we have to gain or lose in the City of Man is like dust on the scales compared to what we have to gain or lose on That Day.

There are a wealth of practical ramifications for having this perspective.

When someone buys something, Paul tells the Corinthians, they are to do so "as if it were not theirs to keep." Or when someone uses "the things of the world," they are to do so "as if not engrossed in them." Why? Because "this world in its present form is passing away" (1 Cor. 7:30–31).

When someone suffers a loss in this world, they can do so without being overwhelmed. The reason, Paul tells the Christians in Rome: "Our present sufferings are not worth comparing with the glory that will be revealed in us" (Rom. 8:18).

The list of examples could go on and on.

The question boils down to this—what will stand the test of That Day? On That Day everything will be shaken except the unshakable City of God. The light will reveal everything for what it really is. The fire will burn up everything not built from imperishable materials. Jesus says the test will be our actions—and what they reveal about our relationship with him. That Day will reveal whether we knew him—or not.

Did we know him? Did we find out what pleases him? Nothing else will matter on That Day.

PUTTING FAITH INTO ACTION

The opportunities for faith-oriented actions are as varied as the people of God. Good works aren't generic but individually planned and prepared in advance for us by the Lord (Eph. 2:10). In every case, it's going to require a certain fixation of purpose to break through the City of Man's enchantments. There usually will be some pain.

SUFFERING LOSS

Robert G. LeTourneau was a mover of dirt. His sixth-grade education didn't stop him from inventing and building the biggest, most efficient, earthmoving machines around. The demand for his machines made him a millionaire many times over. But for LeTourneau the joy wasn't the money. The joy was coming up with a design that solved a problem and made it possible to do huge jobs with minimal effort and in less time. He relished the giant "Tonka" toys he built and the sheer power they contained—power that could clear rocks, dig tunnels, and subdue the earth for human habitation.

Before he became successful, however, LeTourneau struggled with what seemed to him to be a choice between all-out devotion to the Lord or to his machines. He sorrowfully agreed with a friend who told him, "[You serve the Lord] by having a list of good deeds. As fast as you do them every week you check them off and say, 'Now that's over. I can get back to work.'"[8] LeTourneau was convinced that if he loved Jesus, something had to change.

"I had the despairing feeling that I would have to give up my material way of life—the moving of earth, the making of fertile land in the desert, the joy of hard work under God's sun, all the things I had come to find so satisfying."[9] One night at a revival meeting, he knelt at the altar and prayed, "Lord, if you'll forgive me and help me, I'll do anything You want me to do from this day on." "The words were straight from my soul, and God heard me," LeTourneau later said. "I know He heard me, because His glory flooded my soul as I made that prayer. I rose from my knees, knowing that I had really met Him."[10]

LeTourneau went out into the yard that night and said good-bye to his machines. The next morning, he went to see the preacher to ask him how to discover what it was God wanted him to do.

LeTourneau left that meeting in a daze of joy. After he and the preacher had prayed, it seemed clear that God wanted him to be an all-out, earthmoving machine builder. The life-changing idea was that he could cut God in on everything he was doing—he could seek God's advice and guidance, he could depend on God entirely, he could testify to God in everything he did. He could do everything to the glory of God. And he could know that God delighted in R. G. LeTourneau—his creation—subduing the earth.

Olympic medalist Eric Liddle once told his sister that when he ran fast and hard, using the natural gifts God had given him, he felt God taking pleasure in him. LeTourneau came to the same realization. He could do what he loved to do—not for money, not for glory, but to please the Lord.

But first came the trial by fire. Just as Eric Liddle had been willing to withstand the intense disapproval of the City of Man and sacrifice a chance at a gold medal in order to honor God by not running on Sunday, LeTourneau, too, came through the crucible of sacrificing his machines for his love of God. God gave Eric his gold medal, and he gave R. G. LeTourneau his machines—but only after they had proved their love for him. Both men reached the point where they could say to God, "What have I in heaven besides you? And there is nothing I desire on earth but you."

INVESTING RESOURCES

Jesus came to make us sons and daughters of the Father in heaven, who do the things they see the Father doing. Our Father blesses both good and evil persons, Jesus said. The joys of creation are given, not randomly or automatically, but purposefully and personally to every human. It pleases God to see his children doing the same, being his instruments in that work of "common grace." LeTourneau's pleasure in building machines was driven by that purpose. He loved them, not only for the joy of using his God-given gifts, but because they served an end. They benefited the human race.

Motives make the difference between heaven and hell. Citizens of the City of Man seek their own ends. They love the symbols of success. The motivations of the citizens of the City of God, on the other hand, are oriented to the activities of God. A friend described LeTourneau this way: "He does not view money as something to be accumulated for the satisfaction of looking at it and counting it each day to check its increase, nor as a measure of a man's worth. He sees it only as a means to produce the machine his mind has conceived, or as a means to bring men to God. A suit of clothes, to him, is simply a garment for proper dress; his car, a means to bring him to his destination; his plane, a conserver of time; his office (unbelievably unpretentious), a place necessary to carry out the duties of the day. There are no status symbols in his life."

Jesus makes it clear that pleasing him has a lot to do with how we use our resources. We each have a treasure of time, talents and gifts, energy, and material goods. On the day of his return, he will ask for an accounting of what we did with those things. Jesus calls the citizens of the City of God to be employed in his endeavors. We are participants in God's gracious activities—stewards of his resources for the general good of the human race. As the apostle Paul says, "As we have opportunity, let us do good to all men" (Gal. 6:10 RSV).

FRONTLINE INVESTING

This general doing of good has been overshadowed by a more pressing concern, however. If you read the Bible and then ask yourself, "What does the Lord care about?" you would have to answer, "His people." Redemption of his people for the sake of his glory is his driving concern. He paid with his broken body and spilled blood to purchase them—to buy them out of the City of Man and bring them into the City of God through faith in himself. He cares intensely about gathering them in through the preaching of the gospel.

Once they're gathered in, he cares intensely that they grow in holiness, that they become more and more unlike citizens of the City of Man—in their perspective, their affections, their thinking, their ambitions, and their decisions. They are to become more and more like citizens of the City of God.

If we want to have pleased Jesus on the day of his return, we need to get on board with this intensity. We must devote ourselves to his people. All of us in the church are called to the loving task of building each other up in the faith. We live for one another's welfare. Those who name the name of Jesus in the midst of the City of Man belong to us, and we belong to them.

We are all involved in a fishing expedition—in casting the net of the gospel to bring others into the Kingdom.

Living between the cross and That Day means living during "the redemptive emergency," as Richard Lovelace put it.[11] The door is open to safety, but the ax is about to fall. God is speaking an urgent, love-filled and fear-filled Word to the world: "Be reconciled to me!" Declaring the gospel is *the* urgent, pressing task of our times.

And it is the great privilege and calling of each one of God's people to have a part in that purpose.

Bill McGreevy runs a natural gas pipeline company outside St. Louis, Missouri. "It's not very exciting," he says. "It's useful; it serves a good purpose. I believe God is pleased when we do a good job. But the only time it's exciting is when a pipeline blows up, and we're trying to keep that from happening."[12]

The way Bill sees it, his pipeline job is secondary. His primary job is to be involved in the redemptive purposes of God. "I don't know what it would be like if man hadn't sinned and cut himself off from God. Maybe then running a pipeline for his glory would be the main purpose of my life. But as it is, I see my job as a context for meeting people who need to hear the Good News.

"I can remember when I was in management training for Service Master, where I used to work. Everybody, from the president of the company on down, had to go through a training program where you learned to do all the service tasks. One night I was on the same shift as a young college student who was training to be a part-time janitor. We were cleaning a surgical room full of shining stainless steel equipment, and we were both covered head to foot with disposable scrubs. We even had on those surgeon hats and masks. Only our eyes were showing.

"As we cleaned the surgery I started talking to him about the Lord Jesus. He was interested. Before we were through we were kneeling in prayer right in the surgery as he repented and received Christ as Savior. As far as I'm concerned, that's what it's all about. Cleaning the surgery was a good thing to do—I think God was pleased by that activity. But it was completely overshadowed by the job of offering that man redemption. The surgery, the bodies that are repaired there—they're temporary. That man's eternal destiny was much more important. That's the work I have a passion for. That's exciting."

Bill sees his job as a means to an end. In the short run, the end is providing natural gas to people who need it while earning a living to support his family. But, ultimately, the end is testifying to Jesus. The way Bill sees it, everything in life has been subsumed by the cross.

As R. G. LeTourneau ran his business with an orientation to God, God's purposes of redemption began to take more and more of a priority. LeTourneau wanted in on the act. By 1951, 90 percent of his profits were going into a foundation for benevolent purposes. A lot of that money went to fund educational institutions. Yet R. G. wanted to see his big machines not only benefit people materially but spiritually as well.

He came up with a four-step plan to bring this about in the jungles of Liberia: (1) supply the local people with machinery and train them to use and maintain the equipment; (2) establish a model village to give them a concrete vision of an improved standard of living; (3) clear an area of jungle for the production of crops and livestock suited to the locality; and (4) by word and example teach the Christian faith, and through the training of local pastors, spread the Word to the villages in the interior.

It worked, and LeTourneau had the added delight of being forced to create his Jungle Crusher. Seventy-four feet long, twenty-two feet wide, nineteen feet high, weighing two hundred and eighty thousand pounds—it cleared impossibly thick jungle growth to make room for thriving citrus, coffee, and rubber groves. Wycliffe Bible translators asked LeTourneau to bring his four-step project to the jungles of the Amazon in Peru. Both projects are thriving.

HAVING A PLAN

"Joe" lives in a middle-sized Midwestern town.[13] An ordinary sort of guy whose life decisions were usually foregone conclusions, Joe seemed to always go with the flow. Falling in love with his college girlfriend, "Lisa," was as easy as falling off a log. Since neither of them could imagine life without the other, marriage was the obvious thing to do. Going to live in his hometown after college to work at his father's car dealership made sense too. His father retired shortly after Joe started working for him, and so Joe took the reins. The newlyweds bought a ranch-style home and started their family. The business suffered a few bad years, and at one point they weren't sure it would survive. But then things turned around. Joe inherited the business and was able to buy out the other partner. He and Lisa woke up one day and realized they were making a lot of money and had the prospect of making a lot more.

"We were coming home from church one Sunday," Joe remembers, "and as we talked, we realized we needed to have some thought about what to do with this money." For the first time, the prospect of going with the flow rang some warning bells. The obvious thing was to rejoice in their good fortune, buy a bigger house and maybe a few other life-enhancing items, and kick in a little more when the offering plate was passed. Instead, they made some radical decisions.

"We needed to have a plan," Joe says, "and some concrete decisions about how we would live. We looked at the house and we said, 'This house is just fine. Let's not get into the house thing.'" Instead, they began evaluating how to invest their resources for the kingdom of God. They decided to give a graduating percentage as their income grew—10 percent, then 20 percent, then 30 percent, then 40 percent and finally 50 percent of their income toward the spread of the gospel. After taxes, their personal income remained fairly static, but the resources they invested in spreading the Good News abroad in the City of Man grew every year. They focused much of their giving on a ministry that reaches out to high school kids and presents them with the message of the cross.

"The bottom line was that we knew we could either live extravagantly and give modestly, or live modestly and give extravagantly," Joe says. "We decided material things were just stuff. We didn't want to start piling up a bunch of stuff."

Their choice has been a continuing joy. "When I'm here at the dealership slugging away day in and day out running the business, it's been a real help to me because the City of God, the unseen world, has become my treasure. I knew I could easily get sucked into the material pride of the thing and that I needed another motivation. This plan gives me clear direction every day about why I'm running a car dealership," Joe says.

The best year the business ever had was in 1994. That was the year they reached 50 percent. "I just thought, *This is so cool. The Lord is really going to bless me. I'm giving one out of every two dollars,*" Joe remembers. "The next year was the worst year we've ever had, and I was hardly able to give beyond 10 percent. I couldn't do anything right." Joe went through what he calls "purging."

"I came out of the thing just thankful to be doing what I'm doing. God reenergized the whole family. The kids saw me struggle. They understood why we live in the house we live in and have made the decisions we've made. We all really got on board the Kingdom priority together."

HEADING STRAIGHT FOR THE GLORY

Bill McGreavy, R. G. LeTourneau, and Joe and Lisa have employed an "investment strategy" that counts the unseen things as substantial and real—and ultimately valuable. They have taken the resources given to them by God—time, talents, money, energy, employment—and invested them in the things of the Kingdom. They've found out what pleases the Lord, what he's about, and they've gotten on board his agenda.

Their choices have been oriented to the cross of Christ and the day of the Lord. They've had to swim upstream in the City of Man, but, as Jesus made so very clear over and over again, people who make those kinds of choices are no fools. The fool, in the long run, will be the one who operates according to the parameters of the City of Man and ends up with nothing—and worse than nothing.

Just a few days before LeTourneau died, he used some of his remaining strength to ask a friend of his to sing his favorite song from Charles Gabriel's *Simple Songs for Toddlers*: "There is sunshine in my soul today, more glorious and bright than glows in any earthly sky. For Jesus is my light . . . when Jesus shows his smiling face, there is sunshine in my soul."

That's it. That's the glory of the saints—the shining, smiling face of Jesus saying, "Well done, good and faithful servant. Enter into the joy of the Kingdom prepared for you."

"Cain built a city," Augustine said, "but Abel, being a sojourner, built none. For the city of the saints is above, although here below it begets citizens, in whom it sojourns till the time of its reign arrives, when it shall gather together all in the day of the resurrection, and then shall the promised kingdom be given to them, in which they shall reign with their Prince, the King of the ages, time without end."[14]

Chapter 10

Crying "Father"

"The Father will give you whatever you ask in my name."
JOHN 15:16

"Mark" was face down on the carpet in his office.[1] The door was locked. The phone was turned off. The receptionist was instructed not to interrupt. Mark was in serious trouble, and he had to have help—right now—from his heavenly Father.

Intensity could be Mark's middle name. Even his jokes are intense. His blue eyes will nail you as he asks you searching questions about your commitment to God. As a graduate of Dallas Theological Seminary, his intention was to become a pastor. But in spite of his prayers, as Mark explains it, "God never gave me a church." Instead, with no background or educational preparation, he ended up the major stockholder and officer of what became a very lucrative oil and gas company in Oklahoma City.

But the preacher still comes through when you're just sitting in his living room listening to him talk.

"I have no 'arm of the flesh' to depend on when it comes to running this company," he says. And then leaning forward, with the zeal of someone who wants you to understand clearly what he's about to say, he adds, "I have had to run it on my knees before God."

On that particular day in his office, however, his knees did not adequately express his desperation. "That time, I was *on my face*," he recalls with measured emphasis.

The problem Mark faced is a little complex for the uninitiated to understand, but it had to do with the futures market. A man who ran one of Mark's branch offices—we'll call him Phil— had bought in on a deal involving gas futures. Phil had purchased 50 percent, and Mark's company had bought the remaining 50 percent. Later, Phil sold his 50 percent to Mark.

The futures market is very volatile. When the price of gas goes down, the value of futures goes up because there is more room to deal—and the value of the futures Phil had sold to Mark went through the ceiling after the sale.

Phil decided to claim he had never sold them. Because he had access to the files in the branch office, he managed to destroy all the evidence that the sale had actually taken place. Even in a meeting with the lawyers, Phil convincingly stuck with his story. But after the meeting, as he was passing Mark in the hall, he quietly whispered with a little smile, "You haven't got a prayer."

What a mistake!

"I might have chalked it up as a loss and just let it go if he hadn't said that," Mark remembers. Instead, he fell down on his face before God.

"Father God," Mark cried out that day, "Phil said I didn't have a prayer. I may not have anything else, but I have got prayer. Show him that you cannot be mocked. Don't let him get away with this."

"That was a beginning of the wildest ride of my life," Mark says.

From the day of Mark's prayer, the price of gas started going up, and the value of the futures shares started plummeting. This meant Phil's ill-gotten gains went from being worth about seven million dollars to actually being a liability of about seven million. Of course, the same was true for Mark's 50 percent.

With financial disaster imminent, Phil offered to get the lawyers together and sell his shares back to Mark. Mark sensed this was God's hand and so he bought them again, "for pennies," making sure he had all the paperwork well in hand this time.

"The very next day the price of gas started dropping," Mark says, "and within a few months, the shares were worth seven million again."

Mark doesn't tell this story to prove a name-it-and-claim-it approach to wealth. He is the first to tell you that the desire for riches is ruinous. His point is simply this—God is real. He answers prayer. If a son of God is in trouble and he goes to his heavenly Father and asks for help, his Father will hear him. He will not sit idly by. He will rise up and act.

When men come to Mark's weekly businessman's Bible study, the first thing he has them do is make a list of specific prayer requests.

"I tell them, 'Don't make it so general that you won't see the answer when it comes.' Again and again, we are amazed at the answers to prayer. Of course God sifts us in the process. Sometimes our motives are all wrong. I ask these guys, 'Why are you prosperous?'

"When you realize that God is sovereign—that, if you have a lot of resources, it's because of God—it comes as a big shock. You have to wonder, why? Is it so you can have a big building with your name on it for everyone to see? I asked God why he had prospered me, and I got this idea of a tree. I believe God wants me to be like a tree where people can find shade. If one of my employees needs help, I am prosperous for that very reason—so I can help him."

A few years back, Mark founded the Whitefield Society, in Oklahoma City. He and some friends put funds into it anonymously, and the money is distributed to needy people—mostly widows and orphans. Mark believes God has made him an instrument of answered prayer to people in trouble—a tree God has planted and caused to spread its branches and grow for the sake of others.

"God gives absolutely free of charge," Mark says. "I tell the guys who come to the Bible study, 'There is nothing for sale here.' We even buy their breakfast," he adds with just a hint of a smile.

A HOUSE OF PRAYER

Mark's confidence in praying to his Father is a direct consequence of what Jesus did. Jesus was intense the day he went into the temple and chased out the money changers. He was intensely committed to the task his Father had given him to do. The City of Man's marketplace mentality had invaded the place God had designated for the Gentiles to worship him. The "haves" were exacting payment from the "have nots" and maybe doing a little entrepreneurial gouging in the process—inside the outer court of the temple.

The sight propelled Jesus into indignant action. "Get these out of here!" he said. "How dare you turn my Father's house into a market!" (John 2:16). To the astonishment of everyone, he then began to turn over the tables, scatter the coins, and drive the sheep and cattle out of the temple area. "It is written, . . . 'My house will be called a house of prayer,'" he said (Matt. 21:13).

Later, John tells us, his disciples realized that this was a fulfillment of Psalm 69:9: "Zeal for your house will consume me" (John 2:17).

Jesus was zealous—not just to clear out the money changers—but to clear the way for even the unclean Gentiles to come to God as their Father. The quote about the Father's house comes from Isaiah 56:7, and it actually says, "My house will be called a house of prayer *for all nations*" (italics added). In that same chapter God promises to give a name that is "better than sons and daughters" (v. 5) to the very people who had always been kept at arms length by the holiness of God.

That was accomplished—ultimately—not by driving out the money changers but by the body of Jesus given as a sacrifice. Zeal for his Father's house did indeed consume him. And when his body was destroyed, and sin was atoned for, the most unacceptable of us received the right to speak to God as our Father. We're not kept out in the court of the Gentiles anymore. Jesus' death brought us right behind the curtain into the Holy of Holies, where previously only the high priest dared to enter, and then only after being carefully sprinkled with the blood of sacrificed animals.

Because of the blood of Jesus, the Father's house, the City of God, is a place of prayer. A place where we can go boldly into the presence of our Father and talk to him and make our requests to him. The message of the old sacrificial system—Stay back!—has been destroyed and turned into a new message—Draw near!

And not just draw near! And not just draw near and ask! But draw near and ask, *and you will receive!* Ten times in his parting words to us—just before he offered up his body—Jesus used the word *ask*, and every time it was to declare, to promise, to joyously reassure us that God will give. In the City of God, there is no buying and selling. Nothing is for sale. It's all bought and paid for.

THE FATHER'S WILLINGNESS

Yet in spite of all the assurances, we have trouble praying. We instinctively think God is going to deal harshly with us. We don't know what to ask for. We don't know what to say. We flinch. We assume a posture. We grovel. We mouth meaningless words. We're presumptuous. We're bored. Our consciences accuse us. We're overcome with anxiety. Mostly, we just don't pray at all.

The problem is that we can't pray those first two words Jesus taught us: *Our Father*. Once we've got those down, all the rest is easy. "When a man . . . comes," John Bunyan said, "in the strength of the Spirit, and cries, 'Father'—that word spoken in faith is better than a thousand prayers."[2] We can say the words, of course. But if we could say them believing that God is *our* Father and understand what that means, the floodgates of joy would open up.

But we just don't get it. We need help.

It should come as no surprise to learn that our Father has taken care of that problem too. It takes the power—the strength—of the Holy Spirit for us to say "Father" and believe it. Our blindness is an escape-proof prison cell, but the Spirit opens our eyes to catch a glimpse of the shining, delighting face of the Father looking directly at us. The Holy Spirit is the "Spirit of prayer." He gives us a deep, internal, revolutionary understanding of the Father's love. He teaches us to say "Abba, Father" and to know that it's true.

How do we get this essential eye-opening work of the Spirit? "Ask and it will be given to you," Jesus says in Luke 11:9. "Seek and you will find; knock and the door will be opened." "If your son asks [you] for a fish," Jesus reasons with us, "will [you] give him a snake instead? (v. 11). How much more will your Father give the Holy Spirit to those who ask him!" (v. 13b).

The Spirit will pull back the curtain of unbelief and show you what the Father's attitude toward you actually is. He will expose the lies and tell you the truth—that the Father loves you. He loves your friendship. He loves to reveal himself to you. He loves to forgive your sins. He loves to meet your needs. He loves to give you faith. He loves to see his children triumph. He loves to pour out the riches of his grace. He loves to bring you into the intimacy of his secret thoughts. He loves to bring about his purposes in answer to your prayers. He loves your praise and thanksgiving.

How much does he love you? Read the Bible and find out. It says he loves you as much as he loves Jesus! When Jesus was praying to the Father for us, he says, "[You] have loved them *even as you have loved me*" (John 17:23, italics added). He explains that this Father-love is the reason we should expect answers to our prayers: "I am not saying that I will ask the Father on your behalf," Jesus says. "No, the Father himself loves you because you have loved me" (John 16:26–27a).

The fact is that Jesus has brought us into all the delights and privileges of sonship that he himself enjoys with the Father. It is the privilege of sons to receive when they ask. In the midst of the City of Man, there is a select group of people who have God's ear because they have believed in his Son—they are his "set apart" ones, his children.

Thomas Goodwin, a preacher back in the 1600s, wrote to his parishioner Sir Nathaniel Rich to assure him of his privileges as a son of God: "He has furnished us with a private key to that treasure," Goodwin said, "which is otherwise shut up fast to all the world."[3] The key, Goodwin said, is the Holy Spirit, who shows us not only all that God has given us, but how to lay claim to it.

And the treasure? All the riches of his grace.

QUALIFIED BY WEAKNESS

This is how Jim Cymbala describes the little church his father-in-law talked him into pastoring: "A shabby two-story building in the middle of a downtown block on Atlantic Avenue [in Brooklyn]. . . . The ceiling was low, the walls needed paint, the windows were dingy, and the bare wood floor hadn't been sealed in years."[4]

Besides this pitiful facility, there was the pathetic little band of believers who made up the church. The attendance dropped to twenty shortly after Jim started preaching regularly. The only song the pianist knew was "O How I Love Jesus," which they sang every week, sometimes more than once.

Cymbala was untrained as a preacher, young and inexperienced. On top of all this was the pitifully insufficient offering every Sunday and the suspicion that someone was stealing from the collection plate.

About the only thing the church had going for them was *weakness*. As it turned out, weakness was all they needed.

Our weakness, contrary to what we feel at a gut level, does not disqualify us from receiving answers to our prayers. Just the opposite. Whatever we need in order to qualify for God's blessings has been taken care of by Jesus' obedience on our behalf. Now we only need one qualification, the very one we find we can manage—abject helplessness.

"As far as I can see," Norwegian seminary professor O. Hallesby wrote, "prayer has been ordained only for the helpless. . . . A helpless soul says to himself, 'God does not answer me because I do not pray right.' . . . My helpless friend, your helplessness is the most powerful plea which rises up to the tender father-heart of God. . . . A humble and contrite heart knows that it can merit nothing before God, and that all that is necessary is to be reconciled to one's helplessness and let our holy and almighty God care for us."[5]

"Reconciled to his helplessness" pretty much describes Jim Cymbala in the early days of his ministry at Brooklyn Tabernacle.[6] At the end of his first month, the mortgage payment of $232.00

rolled around. There was $160.00 in the church checking account. He prayed, "Lord, you have to help me. I don't know much—but I do know that we have to pay this mortgage."[7]

The next day, when he went into the office, he hoped to find that someone had sent in some money out of the blue. But when the mail came—nothing.

"God," he sobbed, "what can I do? We can't even pay the mortgage." He called out to God for about an hour, and eventually a new thought came. "Wait a minute! Besides the mail slot in the front door; the church also has a post office box. I'll go across the street and see what's there. Surely God will answer my prayer!"[8]

With a bounce in his steps, Jim walked into the post office and checked inside the box—nothing again. "As I stepped back into the sunshine, trucks roared down Atlantic Avenue. If one had flattened me just then, I wouldn't have felt any lower. Was God abandoning us? Was I doing something that displeased him? I trudged wearily back across the street to the little building."

"As I unlocked the door, I was met with another surprise. There on the foyer floor was something that hadn't been there just three minutes before: a simple white envelope. No address, no stamp—nothing. Just a white envelope."[9] And inside—two anonymously given fifty-dollar bills.

This answer naturally encouraged Cymbala that God was near and that he had heard his pleas for help in a wonderful way. However weakness continued to characterize the worship and the preaching. One Sunday night, he remembers, "I was so depressed by what I saw—and even more by what I felt in my spirit—that I literally could not preach. Five minutes into my sermon, I began choking on the words. Tears filled my eyes. Gloom engulfed me. All I could say to the people was, 'I'm sorry . . . I . . . I can't preach in this atmosphere . . . I can't go on. . . . Would the rest of you come to this altar.'"[10]

The people responded to his request and joined Jim at the front while he put his face in his hands and sobbed. "Things were quiet at first," he says, "but soon the Spirit of God came down upon us. People began to call upon the Lord, their words motivated by a stirring within. 'God, help us,' we prayed. A tide of intercession arose. Suddenly a young usher came running down the center aisle and threw himself on the altar. He began to cry as he prayed. Instantly I realized that he was apologizing for taking money from the offering plate."[11]

God's Spirit had come upon them and something very powerful had happened—a secret sinner had come into the light and confessed. Here's the lesson Cymbala says he learned: "That evening, when I was at my lowest, confounded by obstacles, bewildered by the darkness that surrounded us, unable even to continue preaching, I discovered an astonishing truth: God is attracted to weakness. He can't resist those who humbly and honestly admit how desperately they need him. Our weakness, in fact, makes room for his power."

When we realize, like Jim did, that God's answers come when we have no resources, not even spiritual resources—no hope, no faith, nothing but nothing—we come face to face with the reality of God. Prayer is not a subjective willing-into-being of a reality that we want. It's not a magic formula that works when we have all the right ingredients. It is an encounter with the objective God of the universe, the God who has promised to give water to the thirsty.

Our helplessness glorifies God because it makes crystal clear the fact that nothing can account for answers to prayer except the reality of God himself. The City of God is invisible in the midst of the City of Man, but no less real. And the God who meets us there is very real.

Jim says it this way: "We just naturally want to hog the show. But when you're backed up against the Red Sea and you cry out to God and God comes through, who else can you give the glory to? It's just so obvious. I think that's why Jesus chose such losers to be his disciples. When you think of who was there on the day of Pentecost—those men probably smelled like bait. He could have chosen guys who could speak. But he didn't. And not only that, he let them prove themselves to be moral failures. But that sense of being completely inadequate opens you up to receive everything God has for you because you're not fooling yourself. You know you can't do it. And when you see God work, you give him all the glory."

"God's glory," according to Dr. C. John Miller, "is the difference between what we are naturally and what we are by the power of the Spirit."

Cymbala's lessons about God's strength resting on his natural weakness were only just beginning on that Sunday when his sermon ground to a halt and he broke down and cried in frustration. Attendance grew to about sixty after that, but there was still a sense of weakness. "One day I told the Lord that I would rather die than merely tread water throughout my career in the ministry, always preaching about the power of the Word and the Spirit but never seeing it," Jim recalls. "I hungered for God to break through in our lives and ministry."[12]

What Jim was asking for was reality—the reality of God— manifested in a powerful and unmistakable way. Shortly after this prayer, he came down with a cough he couldn't shake and spent some recuperative time with his in-laws in the sun and salt air of Florida. While he was there, he prayed one more time, "Lord, I have no idea how to be a successful pastor. I haven't been trained. All I know is that Carol and I are working in the middle of New York City, with people dying on every side, overdosing from heroin, consumed by materialism, and all the rest. If the gospel is so powerful . . . ."[13] He couldn't finish the sentence.

Then, with unmistakable reality, Jim sensed God reassuring him deep within his spirit. The message was simply this: God would always supply every need for the church; he would continually give Jim a fresh message to preach and manifest the power of the gospel . . . *if* he and his wife Carol would lead the people to pray and call upon his name.

What God promised Cymbala wasn't something new. It wasn't something unique to his situation. It is what he has promised in his Word to all his children. If we ask, acknowledging our inability, God will pour out the Spirit, and we will see things happen.

Cymbala realized that weakness was not something he would recover from some day. "I don't think a prayer life can be sustained except by a feeling of conscious weakness," he says. "There is something about the human ego, our self-dependence, and our independence from God that makes us treat prayer as just 'something I'm supposed to do.' That's not what prayer is in the New Testament. They prayed because they desperately needed God's help; they sensed their own insufficiency. I still go through that. I'm groping as much now as I was back then."

"For instance, right now Carol is at home working with the musicians for a new album. She still can't read or write music. To give birth to her music, she is totally dependent on God. Our sense of need continues to drive us to the Word of God, to his faithfulness, to his promises. Look at the fourth chapter of the Book of Acts, when Peter and John had just been released and they are warned not to speak in the name of Jesus. Instead of just saying 'I can do all things through Christ who strengthens me' like a mantra, or looking back to the day in the upper room when there was fire on their heads, they went to a prayer meeting where they lifted their voices to God for fresh power to meet a fresh challenge."

When we pray that way, Cymbala insists, our expectations from God should be great. Today Brooklyn Tabernacle has more than six thousand in attendance, and from all the evidence, it would appear that the water of the Spirit hasn't dried up yet.

THIRST FOR THE CITY OF GOD

As you read his story, you see Jim Cymbala not only becoming more and more aware of his weakness, but getting thirstier and thirstier for God. Being in the midst of the City of Man, with all its darkness and hopelessness and indifference to the gospel, created a sort of desperate dehydration in him. His own weakness and the weakness of the gospel in the midst of the destructive virility of the City of Man welled up in him like a tide of sorrow. He was thirsty to see God demonstrate the power of the gospel—to triumph in the midst of the City of Man.

He was in good company. "Let not man triumph," the psalmist pleaded with God (Ps. 9:19). "Your kingdom come, your will be done," Jesus taught us to pray (Matt. 6:10). "I would rather die than continue preaching a weak and ineffectual gospel," Cymbala told God. He wanted to see the power of the gospel—here and now. The deacon who repented was a little "firstfruit" answer. The Kingdom was manifest in the way it always is—the Spirit was poured out, people woke up and began to pray with real grief and genuine desire, and bingo! A person was changed! A man came out of the darkness into the light.

But that was just the first trickle. The congregation kept praying, and like Ezekiel's vision, the water level kept rising. God obviously loves that kind of prayer.

The key to answered prayer, it seems, is to get thirsty for the right things.

GETTING THE RIGHT THIRST

James says, "You do not have, because you do not ask God. When you ask, you do not receive, because you ask with wrong motives, that you may spend what you get on your pleasures" (James 4:2–3). Clearly, not every kind of thirst is going to be satisfied by our Father in answer to prayer. There are some thirsts he promises unequivocally to satisfy, but there are others he wants to dry up.

James gives us a pretty broad clue about what these wrong desires are in the very next line of his letter: "Don't you know that friendship with the world is hatred toward God?" (James 4:4).

The City of Man holds out its pleasures—its status, security, possessions, and delights—like a tantalizing drink that mocks the City of God. When our eyes light up—when we say, "Yes, that's what I want!"—we become traitors to the cause of the Kingdom.

The hard reality is that these two cities are at war, and when we buy into the agenda of the City of Man and crave the things it has to offer, we are sellouts. As long as we feast our eyes on the City of Man with relish, the thirst that God promises to satisfy will not be a reality in our prayers. We won't be able to pray along with Jesus as true sons of the Father, "Your Kingdom come, your will be done on earth"! Here! Now! May the power of the gospel of Jesus prevail!

According to Cymbala, God has to put those desires in us. "We don't even have right desires," he says. "We have to go to God and say, 'God, I want the desires and yearnings that you want to put in me.' In Jim Cymbala there is no good thing. Talk about helplessness!

"On my own, I will want things like making Brooklyn Tabernacle famous or seeing things happen so I can brag about them. But when he gives us *his* desires, when we are really motivated by love for people, and by being able to say 'Look what God can do,' then we can pray like 1 John 5:14–15 says: 'If we ask anything according to his will . . . we know that we have what we asked of him.'"

Augustine's father had high City-of-Man ambitions for his son. He wanted the very best in liberal education for him as a stepping stone to greatness and wealth. Consequently, Augustine was trained in the bustling metropolis of Carthage to be a rhetorician—someone who makes their living using a highly developed method of arguing cases and giving speeches.

Augustine succeeded in his chosen field, so much so that he obtained a position in Rome and was eventually appointed the government professor of rhetoric in Milan, where he rubbed shoulders with the most elite and influential people of that time (A.D. 384). Augustine described himself as "hunting after the emptiness of popular praise . . . and the intemperance of desires."[14]

Meanwhile, Monica—Augustine's mother—had a City-of-God agenda for her son. She cried for him to God every day of his life, "more than mothers weep over the bodily deaths of their children," Augustine wrote.

After praying for Augustine's conversion for years, Monica had a dream. She saw herself standing on a wooden ruler with a shining young man coming toward her, smiling. He asked her why she was crying, and she explained that she was grieving for her son's lostness. The young man told her to look and see that where she was standing, her son was also standing. When she looked, she saw Augustine next to her on the same ruler. From the time of that dream until Augustine's conversion—nine years in all—Monica continued to pray for her son, only now with great expectation that God had heard her prayers.

Nine years later, Augustine had come to the point where he was convinced that the Christian faith was true, and he longed to enter the City of God; however, his desire to enter was thwarted again and again by his desire for "carnal concupiscence" (sex) and "worldly things." Finally, the conflict in Augustine's heart reached the crisis stage. One day in the garden outside his home, he cried out to God, "How long? How long? Why not now? Why not end my uncleanness this hour?" In answer, Augustine seemed to hear this message: "Why do you try to stand in your own strength and so not stand at all? Throw yourself on Him and don't be afraid that he will withdraw from you and let you fall. He will receive you and heal you."

In spite of these reassurances, Augustine continued to hesitate. As he cried and prayed, he became aware of children's voices from a neighboring house chanting, "Take up and read. Take up and read." Augustine interpreted this as a command from God. He opened the Epistle of Paul to the Romans and read the first words he saw: "Let us behave decently, as in the daytime, not in orgies and drunkenness, not in sexual immorality and debauchery, not in dissension and jealousy. Rather, clothe yourselves with the Lord Jesus Christ, and do not think about how to gratify the desires of the sinful nature" (Rom. 13:13–14).

That did it. All the struggle and doubt ended as Augustine "clothed himself with the Lord Jesus Christ." Meanwhile, his friend Alypius had been loitering around the garden somewhat alarmed by Augustine's show of emotion. When Augustine explained what had happened, Alypius was also converted, and together they went in to tell Monica. Augustine wrote to God about his mother's reaction in his *Confessions*: "She rejoiced! When we told her how it had happened, she leaped for joy and triumphed and praised You! 'Who are able to do above all we ask or think.' . . . You heard her, you heard her, oh Lord. You heard her and didn't despise her tears. . . . Oh, you good Omnipotent, who so cares for every one of us as if you cared for him only; and so for all as if they were but one!"

RECOVERING FROM APATHY

In Augustine's day, the philosophers lauded a condition they called *apatheia*—a Greek word from which we get our word *apathy*. Since emotions keep a person off balance and unable to live according to pure reason, these men taught that *apatheia*—the state of having no strong emotions—was the ideal state. When Socrates calmly faced his death, he epitomized this passionless attitude.

Augustine, however, took issue with this concept. As long as we are in the City of Man, experiencing the City of God only in part, he argued, "we are rather worse men than better if we have none of these emotions." He referred to Psalm 69 to make his case: "I looked for someone to lament with me, and there was none."

We are going to have these desires and fears and sorrows, Augustine says. The only way we can avoid them is to "blunt our sensibilities." Those who manage to do that, however, have made a bad trade-off because their "superior" emotionless state causes them to be "elated with ungodly pride."[15]

The answer is to have the emotions that are proper to a citizen of the City of God. Don't be apathetic about the Kingdom! Long for it as you make your pilgrimage. Desire it with all of your being. "The citizens of the holy city of God, who live according to God in the pilgrimage of this life, both fear and desire, grieve and rejoice.

And because their love is rightly placed, all these affections of theirs are right."[16]

Psalm 84 says that those whose strength is in God and whose hearts are set on the City of God will pass through the valley and make it "a place of springs" (Ps. 84:6). As you pray to God to satisfy your thirst for him and for his glory and his power and his presence in the midst of the City of Man, the Spirit will be poured out, and living water will spring up. All the promises that God will answer prayer are for those "who have set their hearts on pilgrimage" (Ps. 84:5).

Love the City of God rather than the City of Man, and God will love your prayers. He will enlist you in his cause and act in answer to your requests. He will delight over you as a son who has thrown himself heart and soul into his father's business.

OPEN WIDE YOUR MOUTH

George Muller is well known for operating orphanages—for more than ten thousand orphans—with no visible means of support except prayer. But not everyone knows what prompted him to do it.

In 1832 Muller became pastor of Bethesda Chapel in Bristol, England. As he visited the Christians in Bristol, he began to realize there was a serious problem: "There was no trust in God. No confidence in the truth of that word: 'Seek first the kingdom of God, and His righteousness: and all these things shall be added unto you,'" he wrote.[17]

He talked to men who were working fourteen or even sixteen hours a day at their trade, who felt trapped by the necessity to provide for their families. When Muller suggested they work fewer hours to have time to rest their bodies and feed their souls with Scripture reading and prayer, he invariably met with doubt.

All around him Muller saw Christians living as if they had no Father, no one to care for them. They seemed to believe that God was either unwilling or unable to provide for their needs. They lived like orphans, thinking they had to look out for themselves because there was no one else to do it. Seeking first the kingdom of God sounded irresponsible. The anxieties of life consumed their thought and energy.

Muller was also concerned about businessmen who "brought guilt on their consciences by carrying on their business almost in the same way as unconverted people do."[18] Although they were often filled with regret about this, they felt they couldn't risk the inherent vulnerability of operating in a dog-eat-dog market without playing by the rules. "Rarely," Muller wrote, "did I see . . . a stand made for God, that there was the holy determination to trust in the living God, and to depend on Him, in order that a good conscience might be maintained."[19] Unbelieving pragmatism dictated the direction of their lives. God was unreal, and concern for his Kingdom a luxury they believed they could not afford.

Muller opened his first orphan house to prove that God was real and that believers could "risk" seeking first the kingdom of God. He wanted to give visible evidence of the reality of God's provision—to be able to say, "See this building? See these children? See their clothing? See their nourished little bodies? The Father does this just for the asking. So don't be afraid to make Him the priority in life."

As he put it, "the first and primary object of the work was that God might be magnified by the fact that the orphans under my care are provided with all they need only by prayer and faith, without anyone being asked by me or my fellow-labourers, whereby it may be seen that God is faithful still, and hears prayers still."[20]

The problems Muller saw afflict us today. Transferring our affections to the City of God is not only a matter of turning away from our City-of-Man desires. We also have to believe we can stop worrying, trusting God to provide for our needs. God has given very concrete promises to provide for the necessities of life. His purpose is to set us free from anxiety so we can reorient ourselves and see his blessings poured out.

"Open wide your mouth and I will fill it" says Psalm 81:10. "This word should be continually present to our hearts," Muller wrote.[21]

"Our gracious God speaks here to each one of his children. It is as if he said, 'Now ask much at my hands, look for much from me, bring great requests before me. I am God, and not man, it is the very joy and delight of my heart to give abundantly.' Let us only wait still on him expectantly, perseveringly, for the glory of God, in the name of Jesus, and we shall see how he will fulfill this word."[22]

Chapter 11
Getting Carried Away

"The kingdom of heaven has been forcefully advancing,
and forceful men lay hold of it."
JESUS, MATTHEW 11:12B

"We're going to the river to a healing," the baby-sitter told Harry's father when she picked up Harry for the day. "This particular preacher don't get around this way often."[1]

No one at Harry's house cared where he went, just so he was out of the way, not making noise that jarred their hung-over heads, and not underfoot when the party began again later in the afternoon.

"You'll like this preacher," the baby-sitter told him as they stood in the living room waiting for Harry's father to dig up some change for the trolley. The trolley ride was long and uneventful, and six-year-old Harry slept on the baby-sitter's ample lap most of the way.

When they got to the sitter's house, Harry noticed a nice picture of a man in what looked like a white sheet, with a gold circle around his head, sawing on a board. "Who's that?" Harry asked. Mrs. Connin just stood there a moment with her mouth open— amazed that a boy could have reached his age without knowing who that was. Then she pulled him onto her lap and read him "The Life of Jesus Christ for Readers under Twelve"—cover to cover.

When they got to the river, the young preacher was standing ten feet out where the water came up to his knees. He looked to be about nineteen years old and was dressed in khaki trousers that he had rolled up out of reach of the water.

"If you just came to see can you leave your pain in the river, you ain't come for Jesus,"[2] he was saying to the crowd. Then he lifted up his head and arms and shouted, "Listen to what I got to say, you people! There ain't but one river, and that's the River of Life, made out of Jesus' blood. That's the river you have to lay your pain in, in the River of Faith, in the River of Life, in the River of Love, in the rich red river of Jesus' blood, you people."[3]

Harry thought it was just a joke when Mrs. Connin encouraged him to go down and get baptized. At his house everything was a joke. But as the preacher held him in his arms, he realized nothing the preacher said or did was a joke.

Quietly the preacher spoke to just Harry, "If I baptize you, you'll go to the Kingdom of Christ. You'll be washed in the river of suffering, son, and you'll go by the deep river of life. Do you want that?"

"Yes," Harry said, and he thought, *I won't go back to the apartment then; I'll go down under the river.*

"You won't be the same again," the preacher said. "You'll count."[4]

THE SERIOUSNESS OF THE CITY OF GOD

Harry is a fictional character in an allegory of the kingdom of Christ written by Flannery O'Conner. In the story, he goes ahead and gets baptized, but nothing changes. He just gets taken back home at the end of the day—a little damp—to the same hopeless little apartment where nobody cares about him much, where he doesn't count much. The next morning Harry gets up early and makes his way back to the river. He wants it to take him seriously—to carry him away like the preacher promised. In O'Conner's story, Harry keeps trying until, finally, the waiting current "caught him like a long gentle hand and pulled him swiftly forward and down."

O'Conner's allegories make their point with a shock. The little boy drowns, but the point O'Conner wants to make couldn't be plainer—the Kingdom is really serious. It's not a joke. It's not a place where you just come to leave your pain. It came violently—by the violent suffering of Jesus. And if you want Jesus, if you want the City of God, then you're going to have to get carried away by it. You're going to have to go under and die.

When Jesus said things like "No one who puts his hand to the plow and then looks back is fit for service in the kingdom" (Luke 9:62), or "Remember Lot's wife!" (Luke 17:32), or "Anyone who does not take up his cross and follow me is not worthy of me" (Matt. 10:38), he was saying that the City of God is not something with which you dabble. You have to take the plunge. You have to give yourself.

And it is in the nature of things that the plunge into the river will also violently wrench you out of the City of Man. That violent wrench will feel like death.

The reason it's so hard, so wrenching and scary, is that, unlike little Harry, we are usually in the grip of the City of Man. It has cast its spell over us. Its attitude finds an echoing chord in our souls. Its contempt for the true God, its inexorable judgments about who gets its glory and who feels its contempt, seems like the prevailing reality. Its promise of life has shaped our pursuit, and its threats strike fear in our breasts. Like primitive people, we are terrified of what will happen if we neglect our idols.

It is no idle fear. The fact is, the City of Man is usually not kind to those who refuse to play by its rules. It seems to say, "Cooperate and you'll be rewarded, but fail to conform and . . . well, try it and see." That message is a real and viable threat. Christians have paid an enormous cost for their faith over the past two thousand years. They have experienced everything from gory, public deaths for refusing to recant, to quiet unnoticed deaths, like being passed over for promotions because they didn't entirely conform to the unspoken expectations.

There is a malevolent personality expressing himself in this enmity toward believers. The City of Man's attitude is not an accident. Behind it is someone who hates God and has poured his not insignificant powers into building a kingdom that rebels against God. He offered Jesus all the kingdoms of the world and all their glory if he would only strike a little bargain and worship him instead of God. Jesus refused, and the utter contempt and cruelty of the cross was Satan's retaliation, administered through the subjects of his kingdom.

The cross is the place "outside the camp" where the shunned, the unacceptable, the shameful and inglorious are consigned to live. What's more, Hebrews 13:13 issues a summons to join Jesus there: "Let us, then, go to him outside the camp, bearing the disgrace he bore." That's the death involved in following Jesus. When we join Jesus, we go outside the camp, outside the City of Man, outside the party.

Paul said, "May I never boast except in the cross of our Lord Jesus Christ, through which the world has been crucified to me, and I to the world" (Gal. 6:14). Paul had to give up all his City-of-Man boasting currency when he followed Christ. He was crucified to the world when he joined Jesus outside the camp. He became an object of scorn.

But the world was also crucified to him, he says. The hierarchy of City-of-Man glory didn't exist for Paul anymore. It wasn't what he wanted. He wanted, instead, to be fully identified with Jesus. He wanted to be as Jesus was in the world so he could be as Jesus is in the City of God—to share in Jesus' glory.

Paul had 20/20 vision when it came to the unseen things. He saw the cross as a royal standard snapping in the wind while leading the ranks of the City of God to the promised glory. He saw it as an emblem of victory that overcame the City of Man and overthrew its ruler through the paradox of weakness and suffering. "Our citizenship is in heaven," he wrote to the church at Philippi. "And we eagerly await a Savior from there, the Lord Jesus Christ, who, by the power that enables him to bring everything under his control, will transform our lowly bodies so that they will be like his glorious body" (Phil. 3:20–21).

The men and women chronicled in the eleventh chapter of Hebrews saw the same thing. Each person listed there made a choice between the unseen City of God and the all-too-present City of Man, and in every case the choice involved some loss. But, no matter. They considered themselves aliens and strangers in the City of Man. "Instead, they were longing for a better country—a heavenly one. Therefore God is not ashamed to be called their God, for he has prepared a city for them" (Heb. 11:16).

SEEING THE CROSSROADS

For Charlie Peacock, the context for that death has been contemporary Christian music. Charlie is a well-known artist, producer, and songwriter in the contemporary Christian genre, and recently he's authored a book about a crossroads. Charlie clearly sees a crossroads—where the decision is made to submit to the Kingdom or to keep going down the wide, broad road of the world.

The wide road leads to destruction in the long run. The Kingdom road leads to life—but it can feel like death in the short run.

To Charlie's way of thinking, you can't straddle the two roads. "The crossroads is always about choosing between the kingdoms of the world and the kingdom of the devil," he says.[2]

Charlie points out that Satan tried to strike a deal when he offered Jesus all the kingdoms of the world in all their splendor. Jesus had to make a choice. In fact, we all have to make the same choice. All of us have to decide to worship God rather than the world. The two kingdoms offer mutually exclusive deals. They can't be pursued simultaneously. If you choose to go down the Kingdom road, then you ipso facto must adopt a don't-look-back attitude to the City of Man. You're going to have to say no to the City of Man's idea of glory if you want to sign on for the real glory.

The big call, according to Charlie, is to "think, speak, live and act entirely for Him." Yet that big call is always lived out in the context of a secondary, individualized call. Some of us are called to be cooks, some carpenters, some CEOs. The big call is lived out in the context of our own personal vocation. The details will differ, but the issues will be the same for us all.

In the world of contemporary Christian music—which is Charlie's arena of action—the City of Man creeps in as a fog of marketplace mentality. "Worldliness," Charlie says, "is saying, 'I have to meet the consumer's demands or I can't stay in business.' That's worldliness. The difference between a Christian and a worldly thinker is that a Christian will say it all belongs to the Lord, and if the Lord raises it up or tears it down, it all belongs to the Lord. The Christian life is upside down from the world's ways of thinking. God allows people to fail. God allows people to go out of business. It may be the very best thing that happens to them personally, and it may be the strongest witness that they ever have.

"You have to be open to letting God be God and not constantly try to control everything to make things work all the time. In fact, it may be God's will that they come undone. You have to remember that it was God who allowed Satan to test Job. And it was also God who allowed Job's life to be completely undone. And it was also God who raised him up, who gave him more in terms of material goods than he'd ever had before. That's the Christian reality. That's the kingdom reality. If you try to live and breathe and move outside of that, you're going to fall into worldliness."[3]

So, according to Charlie, getting carried away by the river means you don't do Christian music with success as the operative agenda. That's where the "death" comes in. You leave the issue of City-of-Man success or failure up to God. You operate according to another agenda. You have a different motive for what you're doing.

"It's a big issue," Charlie says. "Most Christian media is supported by the listener or viewer, and they are dependent on giving that supporter what it is they want. But see, that's not a Christian worldview. You don't just give people what they want. You give people what they need. That's the difference between a standard approach to media and a Christian approach. So Christians will just have to determine, 'which line of reasoning do I want to follow?'

"So you follow God's way and you fail by the world's standards. I know someone, Jesus Christ, who followed God's way and failed by the world's standards and ended up hung up on a cross between two thieves."[4]

In recent years, the contemporary Christian music industry has crossed over into the bigger arena of secular media. "People get it now," Charlie says. Christian music is only one more genre in the marketplace, and the media have co-opted and exploited it.

"Unfortunately, what they get is usually a further reduction of our already reduced and marginalized version of Christianity and the kingdom of God. It comes out so incredibly small that the result is like an eight-ounce glass trying to hold the oceans of the world—only a few drops fit."[5]

The cost of finding a place for the river in the City of Man has been to reduce it to a little run-off ditch. In reality, Charlie says, it is so huge that "it involves every action, emotion, and thought under the sun—a complex, bloody, beautiful, redemptive, truthful story."[6]

Retaining the enormity of that story, according to Charlie, will mean abandoning conventional City-of-Man wisdom for the wisdom of the cross. "The wisdom of the cross is foolishness to the world," Charlie says, quoting 1 Corinthians. "Sadly, its grand significance is often lost on Christians as well. Without the wisdom of the cross, the spiritual vision to see what we need to see will constantly elude us. We will see celebrity as the answer, and we will see more quantity as somehow more profitable than less quantity but greater quality. The wisdom of the cross is paradoxical and is upside down from the wisdom of the world."

"What if," Charlie asks, "rather than trying to show the world we can be cool, what if we were to show them we can be fools for things worth being foolish for? Perhaps God would be present in our shame, our humility, our powerlessness and our folly."[7]

That, after all, is the way of the cross. It's not something we adapt to the dictates of consumerism. It's a river we drown in.

WALKING AWAY FROM THE TABLE

When Augustine was not yet converted, he heard a story that made him long to lose himself for the City of God. He had a great deal to lose, but Victorinus had more.[8]

Like Augustine, Victorinus was a professor of rhetoric but his reputation in the City of Man far exceeded Augustine's. Victorinus taught rhetoric to the Roman senators. He was a venerable, aged man—honored with no less symbol of glory than a statue of himself in the Roman Forum—when he began to read the Scriptures. He, who had spent his life defending the deities with "thundering eloquence," was captivated by what he read about Jesus.

"He most studiously sought and searched into all the Christian writings," said Simplicianus, who told the story to Augustine. The day came when Victorinus quietly informed his good friend Simplicianus in strictest confidence, "I am already a Christian." But Simplicianus told him, "I will not believe it, nor will I rank you among Christians, unless I see you in the Church of Christ."

"Do walls then make Christians?" he shot back at Simplicianus. The reason for his shyness was blatantly obvious: "He feared to offend his friends . . . from whom he supposed the weight of enmity would fall upon him."

But Simplicianus knew that we can't have it both ways. We have to take the plunge if we want Jesus. Eventually Victorinus saw it that way too. As he studied the Scriptures, he realized with growing conviction that he would make Jesus ashamed of him before his Father if he was ashamed of Jesus before the City of Man.

This is how Augustine tells it: "He appeared to himself to be guilty of heavy offense, for being ashamed of the Sacraments of the humility of the Word, and not being ashamed of the sacrilegious rites of those proud demons whose pride he had imitated." Suddenly and unexpectedly he said to Simplicianus, "Go we to the church; I wish to be made a Christian."

The leaders of the church offered to let Victorinus profess his faith privately, but he refused. Everyone in the church was amazed when he went forward and, as Augustine relates it, "All wished to draw him into their very heart; yes, by their love and joy they drew him there."

Rome was also amazed, and then full of fury. The upper echelon couldn't get rid of him fast enough. Their contempt for him had no bounds. In the days of Emperor Julia, a law had passed forbidding Christians to teach the liberal sciences or oratory, and so Victorinus lost not only the esteem of Rome but his livelihood as well.

When Augustine saw the glory of Victorinus's choice, it deepened his misery that he hadn't the courage to do the same. In the end, Victorinus's courage helped give Augustine the push he needed.

The City of Man had spread a banquet table of delights in front of Victorinus, but he chose to walk away from the table. He preferred to eat from another table, and the choice involved a cross. He suffered an acute loss when he suddenly found himself "outside the camp." But, as Augustine wrote from his own experience, "everywhere the greater joy is ushered in by the greater pain."

BEING LAST

Since Joseph Wheat came to Village Seven Presbyterian Church one year ago, the church has sprung to life.[9] Already the largest church in the denomination west of the Mississippi, membership has grown by leaps, and everyone hangs on young Pastor Wheat's words from the pulpit. He laughs uproariously, he cries unashamedly, he loves unreservedly, and he passionately preaches the gospel. The impact can be seen on the faces in the congregation. They're beginning to mirror their new pastor and shine with joy and enthusiasm.

Wheat chuckles as he confides that his sudden "success" has catapulted him into the spotlight: "Now all these big Christian ministries want me to be on their board." There's a glow around Wheat, and people want to get close to him. He's in demand by other ministries because of his growing status in Christian circles. He's definitely an up-and-comer from a christianized City-of-Man point of view, and the temptation to feast on the glory is right at his door. Wheat explains:

> As seductive as that is, I have to say no. I wake up every morning and look in the mirror, and I am still the same sinner who has to struggle with my own pride that day. My halo has not appeared yet. It is a miracle that I am even a Christian. If you had known me before, you'd understand. And the fact that God has called me to serve him is an even bigger miracle. But I don't see the larger things as any bigger than the smaller things.
>
> Let me tell you an early life-shaping story. When I was in seminary, I became the guy everybody wanted. I remember the placement office in the seminary was a gathering place for last-year students. They were all worried about getting a job. I could feel the anxiety and the urgency to get a place, and a lot of us were competing for the same positions. It was a tough deal emotionally. I was single and really wasn't too worried. And then one day a fellow student said to me, "You don't have to worry. You have an outgoing personality and you're this and this and this," and he listed all these assets, and then he said, "You'll be one of the first people to get a job out of our class, and you'll get one of the best jobs."
>
> It kind of took me by surprise. But it was a defining moment. I thought, and I'm embarrassed to say this, but I thought, *He's right.* In my heart I just owned that comment. And it seemed like those words were almost prophetic. I was recruited to a church-planting situation that was a plum. They wooed me and wanted me and I accepted the position.

But then this is what happened. After the school year was over and all the good jobs were filled, I got this phone call from this church, and the man said, "Joseph, I've got bad news for you. We've changed our mind. We've just prayed about it, and we think we need a married man."

Let me tell you something. I was living with a friend in the middle of the winter without heat. I got sick, and I was sitting on the concrete floor throwing up in a bucket. I was angry with God. I mean, I was low.

But I truly believe God was making a point with me that he didn't want me to ever forget. Because when I finally got a position, I was the *last* person in my class to be placed. Not second to the last, but last. And the job I took was one that I had turned down early on in the process. It was a job as a singles pastor, and I had told them, "I'm not going to baby-sit your singles." I had thought I was destined for bigger things.

This is what I learned: "I am the vine, and you are the branches. Apart from me you can do nothing." I mean, I *learned* it. This idea that God is blessed to have me on his team is no longer a part of my thinking. Nobody even missed me during those wretched months. The kingdom of God went on. By the time I got to my new job, there has never been a person more thankful to be able to serve in God's kingdom. God worked in me so that all I wanted was to be faithful to do the job he gave me to do in the kingdom. It doesn't matter if it's big or small.

Joseph Wheat consciously resists the temptation to take his place at the head of the table. He knows by experience what it feels like to have the Master move him down to the lowest place. "The first will be last" is a working concept in Joseph's life.

INVESTING CURRENCY

Henry and Susan Crowell were heavy with City-of-Man currency. As Crowell's biographer put it, "It seemed that Henry amassed enormous wealth without even trying."[10]

Henry Crowell was always a step ahead of the crowd, gifted with providential timing, visionary imagination, and entrepreneurial genius. Even his defeats seemed to effortlessly turn into successes. He founded the Quaker Oats Company and revolutionized the American breakfast with his nutritious boxed breakfast foods. At the same time he impressed "even the biggest and most cynical movers and shakers of the world of commerce, less for the wealth he had amassed than for his work ethic, character and charity."

For much of his life Crowell practiced the kind of Christianity that doesn't make enemies in the City of Man. His commitment to Christ was genuine, his integrity unimpeachable, and his giving to charity at about the 70 percent level. But his religion stayed within the bounds accepted—even lauded—by the City of Man.

Then in the fall of 1889, a Bible study began to meet in the Crowell home at Susan's suggestion, and it changed their lives. Until then, Susan had practiced her faith as a normal part of moral respectability the world expected in the late 1800s. However, when Dr. William Newell conducted his Bible studies, things suddenly became serious. Susan was brought face to face with the reality of sin and the need for salvation, and she responded wholeheartedly. She was transformed from a nominal, "dabbling" Christian to someone who heard the call to live and act entirely for Jesus everywhere and in everything.

Henry's faith was rocked and energized by Susan's conversion and by Dr. Newell's serious study of God's Word. Newell treated the Scriptures more like food and drink than a source of inspirational devotionals. Henry began to consume the Bible.

It wasn't long before the Crowells realized that their new faith was something the City of Man doesn't tolerate gladly. Susan's conversion became the talk of the so-called "Gilded 400"—Chicago's official list of top-of-the-heap society families. In place of the society balls and parties, Susan's life began to revolve around her church and helping less fortunate people. Her former companions were embarrassed and uncomfortable, and the Gilded 400 started looking "for ways to gracefully drop the Crowells off their guest lists." Above all, no one wanted to be invited to the Crowell home where the conversation was all too likely to turn to God.

Henry and Susan had a clear-eyed grasp of their position in the City of Man. They knew they had lost some currency in the eyes of the social elite, but their investable resources were still huge.

As Susan continued to host home Bible studies, Henry began sharing his faith in his business circles. Over one lunch at the prestigious Union League Club, he spent the entire time telling his friend and associate William Robinson about Christ. Robinson later reported on the meeting: "One by one my objections fell away. Henry was quite persuasive. I decided, then and there, as I would answer any corporation question, to come to God. From that day I have been a new creature in Christ Jesus. . . . All my doubts, skepticism . . . were swept away. I went back to my office and told my closest associate. He listened to what had happened to me, and he grasped my hand and told me, 'I want that, too. I'll start with you!'"[13]

Henry's calendar was soon filled with luncheon meetings and office chats about spiritual matters. He had a new, unstratified view of people, which led him to disregard their status in the City of Man. He began to spend as much time with elevator operators, assembly line workers, and floor sweepers as he spent with his fellow tycoons.

Henry also exerted his considerable influence to pass legislation shutting down the most notorious houses of prostitution in Chicago. He applied his business acumen and financial resources to put Moody Bible Institute on its feet. Henry then saw the potential of radio for spreading the gospel, and he forged the path for WMBI—a state-of-the-art radio station totally devoted to the message of Christ.

Susan and Henry Crowell saw the river and they dove in head first, investing their considerable City-of-Man currency in the cause of the gospel. If they struggled with the decision, there's no record of it. That it cost them is certain, but they saw the reward—the City with foundations, whose Architect and Builder is God.

CHOOSING GOALS

Bud Wilson—chairman of the board of Bocar Industries, a one-hundred-million-dollar-per-year food brokerage company in Indianapolis—exemplifies focus.[11] Intense and fast talking, Bud wastes little time on small talk. The more than forty stray dogs he and his family have adopted reflect the kind of wholehearted intensity that shows up in all of Bud's endeavors.

"Every day," Bud explains with no preamble, "you have to decide: What is your goal? Management has learned to adopt a team approach to increase productivity. Some even model themselves after Jesus, who chose twelve close associates, trained them personally, invested them with his vision, and sent them out two by two. But they've adopted his methods to achieve City-of-Man goals. They're just managing the world's agenda.

"Every day I have to decide: What is my goal? Everyday I have to say, 'Lord, have your way with me. Your goal is my goal.' And what is his goal? What was Jesus' goal when he sent out his disciples? To bless people and call them to himself.

"We've watered down the call to make it fit our schedule. We think it shouldn't cost us anything. But Jesus didn't leave room for that. He told us, 'The world will hate you.' You just have to decide—will his goals be my goals regardless of the cost? Because it will cost. We have the world's pressure on us all day, every day.

"I stumble when I forget to stop and pray and read the Bible. Then I just automatically fall into the City of Man's decision-making process. I have to stop and decide, every day—my goal is Jesus' goal—to bless people and call them to him."

For Bud that call is very practical. It means being available and willing to obey throughout the day. It means being alert to interruptions that wreck his schedule, to stop and respond to someone who needs him very badly—even if it might cost him money. As Bud puts it, "You just take up your cross. It's usually a sacrifice of some sort in the City of Man's economy. But it's all glory and joy in the City of God."

A case in point was the purchase of the food service side of another large brokerage firm. The owner was desperate—at age forty-nine, after investing a lifetime building up the business, he had contracted Lou Gehrig's disease. He was in no position to bargain and was willing to let go of his business list for 5 percent of the profits. Instead, Bud gave him 20 percent with the first three years projected profits up front.

"I told him," Bud says, "'I wouldn't have made that decision if Jesus Christ wasn't Lord of my life.' I just had to ask, 'How can I focus on Jesus' goal to bless this man? I can't serve money and Jesus at the same time. I just had to do it and figure the losses are part of the cross."

Bud talks with a forceful vehemence that gives testimony to the violence it takes to enter the Kingdom. It's not easy to take the daily plunge. As Bud says, "Every day you have to give yourself over to the Holy Spirit for God's purposes. You have to say to yourself, every day—This is my goal—Don't love the world—Die to yourself—Submit to Christ."

FINISHING WELL

Dr. James Maxwell was definitely an honored guest at the party of the City of Man.[12] His lifelong practice of gynecology and obstetrics in Colorado Springs had gained him a waiting-list practice, an exclusive home above the Garden of the Gods with a striking view of Pikes Peak, and the undying gratitude of countless women.

But Maxwell was restless. It was all a little too comfortable, a little too easy. Three years ago he had gone to his college alumni meeting and met a new friend, a fellow Christian and physician in charge of the medical side of a mission organization. He suggested to Maxwell that he fill the vacancy of a missionary who had been a public health officer in Cambodia.

Maxwell was intrigued, but he couldn't imagine actually doing it. The opportunity came and went, but the idea of serving somewhere other than the affluent United States stuck with him.

"I think my dissatisfaction with the way medicine is practiced in this country was an instrument God used to keep me thinking about a radical change. Doctors are no longer professionals; they're technicians. Algorithms on computers have become the decision makers. Insurance companies decide if a treatment is financially viable. Medicine has become a business in this country. It's not about human relationships anymore.

"I knew that there were thirty other doctors in Colorado Springs who could treat my patients at least as well as I could. I thought, *If I leave town it won't cause a ripple*. But people in the Third World are desperate for what I can offer."

But the leaving wasn't easy. In fact, it was almost impossible to pull away from his practice. It was like swimming upstream in molasses. There seemed to be an indefinable resistance holding him back. He was caught in a kind of inertia, until he remembered a conversation with Bible teacher Walt Hendrikson.

In the course of that conversation Hendrikson had said, "I know a lot of guys on fire for the Lord in their twenties, thirties, forties, and fifties. But I know only a handful still on fire in their sixties and seventies."

When Maxwell remembered that conversation, he had just passed his sixty-eighth birthday. "I was deeply challenged," he said. "I did not want to finish poorly."

Then Maxwell heard about a need in a hospital in Honduras for someone with his training. A few months later he and his wife visited the country. "We knew that was what God wanted us to do." They went home and started the long difficult process of extricating themselves from a lifetime of involvements and eventually arrived at Hospital Evangelico in Siguatepeque, Honduras, where Maxwell began practicing medicine without pay.

A few weeks after they arrived, Hurricane Mitch hit Honduras with a vengeance, and the country was devastated—except in the central part where Maxwell was practicing. After the winds died down, his hospital was the only one in the country still fully operational, and they worked night and day for weeks distributing aid and medical care.

Things have settled down now, and Maxwell is busy with his normal clinic practice. They show the *JESUS* film in the waiting room where about a half dozen people come to the Lord each month. Maxwell says the nurses exude the love of Jesus. People with real need and no resources are getting quality care, and Maxwell feels like a doctor again.

"I'm excited," he says. "I know the world operates on the principle 'the one with the most toys wins.' There's no question that this doesn't have anything to do with what really matters in God's economy. In his economy, when it's all said and done, only love remains. When we see God, that's what will be real. That's what will have value. I have been challenged to the core of my being to finish well."

LOOKING FORWARD TO THE CITY

The Hebrews 11 list goes on—citizens of the City of God who have been carried away by the river of Jesus' blood, people who have thrown themselves into the river because Jesus threw himself into the river for them. They are his people, people he has rescued from the kingdom of darkness and brought into the Kingdom of light.

They are a people who have the cross as their emblem of victory, who overcome the City of Man with the blood of the Lamb, and the word of their testimony—who do not love their lives so much as to shrink from death. They live by faith, certain of the things not seen. Like Abraham, they are strangers in the world, "looking forward to the city with foundations, whose architect and builder is God" (Heb. 11:10).

C. S. Lewis wrote an essay he called "The World's Last Night," and in it he made the case that we cannot possibly know when the sudden end of the City of Man will come and the visible, consummated City of God will be established, but we can know what we would like to be found doing when it does come.

"In King Lear," he wrote, "there is a man who is such a minor character that Shakespeare has not given him even a name: he is merely 'First Servant.' All the characters around him—Regan, Cornwall, and Edmund—have fine long-term plans. . . . The servant has no such delusions. He has no notion how the play is going to go. But he understands the present scene."[13]

In his one scene, First Servant is standing in attendance when he realizes that his master is about to put out the eyes of an old man who has done nothing wrong. He reacts immediately and tries to stop the injustice. In an instant, another character stabs him in the back and he falls down dead. That's it. That's his part—eight lines in all.

"But if it were real life and not a play," Lewis said, "that is the part it would be best to have acted."[14]

There are no small parts in the drama of the world's history. They may look small from the City of Man's point of view, however, as Howard Butt puts it, "God makes big worlds little and little worlds big; obedience is the secret; there are no little places anywhere."[15]

And the reward is no small thing either!

"The saints have their dominion, their glory, their greatness, their victory, their splendor," Pascal wrote, "and have no need of carnal or intellectual greatness which has no relevance to their domain, for it neither adds to nor detracts from it. They are seen by God and the angels, not by bodies or curious minds. God suffices them."[16]

God suffices them in the midst of the City of Man, and when the world has finally seen its last night, they will "shine like the sun in the kingdom of their Father."

Notes

PREFACE

1. Jacques Ellul, *The Presence of the Kingdom* (Colorado Springs, Colo.: Helmers and Howard Publishers, Inc., 1989), 33, 34.

CHAPTER 1: GOING FOR THE GLORY

1. Quotations are from interviews with Jeffrey Comment and from his book: Jeffrey Comment, *Mission in the Marketplace* (N. Kansas City, Mo.: MITM Publishing, 1995).

2. Martin Luther, *Luther's Works, Volume I*, ed. Jaroslav Pelikan (St. Louis, Mo.: Concordia Publishing House, 1958), 315.

3. Augustine, *The City of God*, trans. Marcus Dods (New York: Random House, Inc., 1993), 477.

4. David Wells, *Losing Our Virtue* (Grand Rapids, Mich.: Wm. B. Eerdmans Publishing Co., 1998), 104.

5. C. S. Lewis, *The Weight of Glory and Other Addresses* (Grand Rapids, Mich.: Wm. B. Eerdmans Publishing Co., 1998), 104.

6. Ibid., 65.

7. Abraham Maslow, *Motivation and Personality* (New York: Harper & Row, Publishers, Inc., 1970), xii.

8. Ibid., 155.

9. Ibid., 158.

10. Ibid., 162.

11. Augustine, *The City of God*, 460.

CHAPTER 2: GETTING LEVELED

1. Quotations are taken from interviews with Gary Grauberger.

2. C. S. Lewis, *The Screwtape Letters* (West Chicago, Ill.: Lord and King Associates, Inc., 1976), 27.

3. Blaise Pascal, *The Mind on Fire*, ed. James M. Houston (Portland, Oreg.: Multnomah Press, 1989), 68.

4. Abraham Maslow, *Motivation and Personality* (New York: Harper & Row, Publishers, Inc., 1970), 167.

5. Ibid., 174.

6. Augustine, *The City of God*, trans. Marcus Dods (New York: Random House, Inc., 1993), 630.

7. A. W. Tozer, *The Pursuit of God* (Camp Hill, Pa.: Christian Publications Inc., 1982), 56.

CHAPTER 3: LEARNING TO SEE

1. C. Everett Koop, *Koop* (New York: Random House, Inc., 1991), 83.

2. Unless otherwise referenced, quotations are taken from interviews with C. Everett Koop.

3. Koop, *Koop*, 86.

4. Ibid.

5. Joni Eareckson Tada and Steven Estes, *When God Weeps* (Grand Rapids, Mich.: Zondervan Publishing House, 1997), 153.

6. Ibid., 105.

7. C. Everett and Elizabeth Koop, *Sometimes Mountains Move* (Wheaton, Ill.: Tyndale House Publishers, Inc., 1979), 12.

8. Tada and Estes, *When God Weeps*, 125.

9. "Pat" and "Linda" are real people who preferred to remain anonymous. The quotations are from an interview with Pat.

CHAPTER 4: LEANING HARD

1. Steven Berglas, "Entrepreneurial Ego," *Inc.*, June 1998, 43.

2. Quotations are taken from an interview with Doug Cobb.

3. Illustration found in Dr. James Montgomery Boice's commentary, *Philippians* (Grand Rapids, Mich.: Zondervan Publishing House, 1979), 131.

4. James Montgomery Boice, *Two Cities, Two Loves* (Downers Grove, Ill.: InterVarsity Press, 1996), 48.

5. "Cecilia" and "Daniel" are real people who preferred to remain anonymous. Quotations are taken from interviews with Cecilia.

6. Friedrich Nietzsche, *The Will to Power*, trans. Walter Kaufmann and R. J. Hollingdale (New York: Vintage, 1967), 96.

7. Quotations are taken from an interview with Gina Cobb.

8. Quotations are taken from an interview with Bob Byers.

CHAPTER 5: BEING RIGHTEOUS

1. Quotations are taken from interviews with John Weiser.

2. Victor Hugo, *Les Misérables* (New York: Penquin Putnam, Inc., 1987), 106.

3. Ibid., 110.

4. Susan Nikaido, "I Must Confess," *Discipleship Journal*, May/June 1997, 8.

5. Quotations are taken from a testimony given by Chuck DeBardeleben during the Presbyterian Church of America General Assembly.

CHAPTER 6: GOING UNDER

1. Howard Butt, *The Velvet-Covered Brick* (New York: Harper and Row, Publishers, 1973), 2.

2. Ibid., 39.

3. Quotations are from interviews with Jeffrey Comment and from his book: *Mission to the Marketplace* (N. Kansas City, Mo.: MITM Publishing, 1995).

4. John Beckett, "Principles and Interest," *The Christian Businessman,* July/August 1998, 23.

5. Augustine, *Britannica Great Books, Vol. 18*, ed. Robert Maynard Hutchins (Chicago: Encyclopedia Britannica, Inc., 1952), 520.

6. Ibid.

CHAPTER 7: LIVING DELIBERATELY

1. Quotations taken from the Internet: www.slowfood.com, December 1999.

2. Unless otherwise referenced, quotations are from an interview with Richard Swenson.

3. Richard Swenson, *Overload Syndrome* (Colorado Springs, Colo.: NAVPRESS, 1998), 13.

4. Ibid., 14.

5. Quotations are from interviews with Lamar Allen and one of his employees.

6. Mrs. Howard Taylor, *Behind the Ranges* (London, Redhill: Lutterworth Press and the China Inland Mission, 1944), 108.

7. Augustine, *Britannica Great Books, Vol. 18*, ed. Robert Maynard Hutchins (Chicago: Encyclopedia Britannica, Inc., 1952), 632.

8. Quotations are from Truett Cathy's book, *It's Easier to Succeed Than to Fail* (Nashville, Tenn.: Thomas Nelson, Inc., Publishers, 1989).

9. Joni Eareckson Tada and Steven Estes, *When God Weeps* (Grand Rapids, Mich.: Zondervan, Publishing House, 1997), 181.

10. Elizabeth Goudge, *The Dean's Watch* (Ann Arbor, Mich.: Servant Publications, 1960), 123.

CHAPTER 8: WEIGHING TRUTH

1. C. S. Lewis, *The Screwtape Letters* (New York: Touchstone, 1961), 19.

2. Quotations are from interviews with Richard and Harriet Segal.

3. The Meloon's story is related in James Vincent's book *Parting the Waters* (Chicago: Moody Press, 1997), 54.

4. Quotations are from interviews with Charles Canady.

5. C. John Miller, *Repentance and Twentieth-Century Man* (Fort Washington, Pa.: Christian Literature Crusade, 1975), 122–24.

CHAPTER 9: TAKING ACTION

1. Ian H. Murray, *D. Martyn Lloyd-Jones, the First Forty Years* (Edinburgh: The Banner of Truth Trust, 1982), 44.

2. Ibid., 93.

3. Ibid.

4. A. W. Tozer, *The Pursuit of God* (Camphill, Pa.: Christian Publishers, Inc., 1983), 15.

5. *Britannica Great Books,* vol. 18, Robert Maynard Hutchins, ed. (Chicago: Encyclopedia Britannica, Inc., 1952), 397.

6. C. S. Lewis, *The Weight of Glory and Other Essays* (Grand Rapids, Mich.: William B. Eerdmans Publishing Co., 1977), 7.

7. Ibid., 10.

8. The R. G. LeTourneau story is related in his book: *R. G. LeTourneau: Mover of Men and Mountains* (Chicago: Moody Press, 1972), 108.

9. Ibid.

10. Ibid.

11. Richard Lovelace, *Dynamics of Spiritual Life* (Downers Grove, Ill.: InterVarsity Press, 1979), 147.

12. Quotations are from interviews with Bill McGreevy.

13. "Joe and Lisa" are real people who prefer to remain anonymous.

14. Augustine, *Britannica Great Books, Vol. 18*, Robert Maynard Hutchins, ed. (Chicago: Britannica, Inc., 1952), 398.

CHAPTER 10: CRYING "FATHER"

1. "Mark" is a real person who preferred to remain anonymous.

2. John Bunyan, *Prayer* (Grand Rapids, Mich.: Sovereign Grace Publishers), 7.

3. Thomas Goodwin, *The Return of Prayer* (Grand Rapids, Mich.: Sovereign Grace Publishers), 1.

4. Jim Cymbala with Dean Merrill, *Fresh Wind, Fresh Fire* (Grand Rapids, Mich.: Zondervan Publishing House, 1997), 11.

5. O. Hallesby, *Prayer* (Minneapolis, Minn.: Augsburg Publishing House, 1975), 16.

6. The story of Jim Cymbala's early days at Brooklyn Tabernacle are found in his book *Fresh Wind, Fresh Fire*, 17–38.

7. Ibid., 16.

8. Ibid., 16–17.

9. Ibid., 17.

10. Ibid., 18.

11. Ibid., 18–19.

12. Cymbala and Merrill, *Fresh Wind, Fresh Fire*, 23.

13. Ibid., 25.

14. This story of Augustine's conversion can be found in his *Confessions: Britannica Great Books, Vol. 18*, ed. Robert Maynard Hutchins (Chicago: Encyclopedia Britannica, Inc., 1952).

15. Ibid., 384.

16. Ibid., 383.

17. Roger Steer, *The Spiritual Secrets of George Muller* (Wheaton, Ill.: Harold Shaw Publishers, 1985), 14.

18. Ibid., 16.

19. Ibid., 15.

20. Ibid., 16.

21. Ibid., 95.

22. Ibid.

CHAPTER 11: GETTING CARRIED AWAY

1. Flannery O'Conner, *The Complete Short Stories* (London: Faber & Faber, 1990), 158.

2. Ibid., 165.

3. Ibid.

4. Ibid., 168.

5. Charlie Peacock, *At the Crossroads* (Nashville, Tenn.: Broadman & Holman Publishers, 1999), 3.

6. Charlie Peacock, "At the Crossroads," *Wireless*, May/June, 1999, 10.

7. Ibid., 11.

8. Charlie Peacock, *At the Crossroads* (Nashville, Tenn.: Broadman & Holman Publishers, 1999), 119.

9. Ibid., 120.

10. Ibid., 155.

11. The story of Victorinus can be found in Augustine, *Confessions: Britannica Great Books, Vol. 18*, ed. Robert Maynard Hutchins (Chicago: Encyclopedia Britannica Inc., 1952), 53–54.

12. Quotations are from an interview with Joseph Wheat.

13. The story of Henry Crowell can be found in his biography: Joe Musser, *Cereal Tycoon* (Rockford, Ill.: Quadras Media, Publishing, 1997), 123.

14. Ibid., back cover.

15. Ibid, 120.

16. Ibid., 121.

17. Quotations are from an interview with Bud Wilson.

18. Quotations are from an interview with James Maxwell.

19. C. S. Lewis, *The World's Last Night and Other Essays* (New York: Harcourt Brace Jovanovich, 1960), 104.

20. Ibid., 105.

21. Howard Butt, *The Velvet-Covered Brick* (New York: Harper & Row, Publishers, 1973), 165.

22. Blaise Pascal, *Mind on Fire* (Portland, Oreg.: Multnomah Press, 1989), 16.